The Monkey Wrench Dad

*Dispatches from the
Backyard Frontline*

Ken Wright

Raven's Eye Press

Raven's Eye Press
Durango, Colorado
ravenseyepress.com

Wright, Ken
        The monkey wrench dad: dispatches from the backyard
        frontline/Ken Wright
        p. cm.

1. Nature Writing
2. Environment
3. American Southwest
I. Title

Library of Congress Control Number: 2008924556
ISBN 978-0-9816584-0-7

Cover art by Bryan Peterson
Book and cover design by Lindsay James, elle jay design
Author photo: Scott Moore

Printed in the United States of America

1 3 5 7 9 10 8 6 4 2

Find out more about Ken Wright at monkeywrenchdad.com.

For Dick & Jean and Frank & Carol

Beaux —
Here's to working
hard to stay feral —
and keep the lands wild —

Ken Wylie
6/08

CONTENT

Preface

Doing It

Hunting the World

Excellent Adventures

Among the Tribe

Postface

Preface

The love of a man for his wife, his child,
of the land where he lives and works,
is for me the real meaning of mystical experience.
Edward Abbey

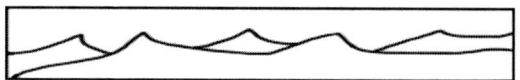

Down the River with Edward Abbey

I am healed! Praise the Gorge!
Or the canyon, anyway. The canyon of the San Juan River to be exact.

We've been on the water for only a half an hour. Our four-boat flotilla has just passed under the forlorn steel span connecting the desert outback of Mexican Hat, Utah, with the butte and mesa wayback of Dinetah, the Navajo Nation. Once it's behind us, the arcing highway bridge swallowed by the canyon corner, we know we have entered the 65-mile-long meandering trench that will contain us for the next five days. And just this knowledge – no, this bodily awareness, this sensual sensibility – is enough to displace the accumulated detritus and flotsam of daily life, the ennui and tedium and fatigue of the routine tasks and distractions of our fussy times and fabricated world. Back there.

For me, there is no more powerful medicine for our civilized afflictions than the slow silty slide of the snaky San Juan through its great sandstone gorges. And those gathered with me here at the river – my teen-age son sitting on the front of my cataraft, my wife and daughter orbiting us in duckies, and our friends and their kids smattered up and down the river in boats and duckies of their own – know what I'm talking about.

Which is why we on this river trip today launch every summer together with a voyage down the San Juan River. It's a tribal celebration, a seasonal ritual, an annual rite of re-passage for all of us to remind ourselves what's important, what's really real. And for the kids, because we've been doing this trip every year since they were each a year old, the San Juan is their summer camp: that intimate place they revisit with their friends year after year, accumulating memories, experiences, challenges, confidence, tallying the most magical seasons of their childhoods.

Please note that in this case I mean "summer" as defined not by the calendar's demarcation; or not even celestially, signifying the solar stand-still at its rolling apogee. I mean "summer" as a lifestyle, an attitude, a perspective, a way of being, or even as just a "way," in the Buddhist sense: Summer-dō. I mean "summer" like how kids mean it – out of school. I mean summer as that time of year that must be devoted to those other, less civilized but equally vital and infinitely older chores: the toughening of one's feet, the tanning of one's torso, and the exploring of the world, out there, beyond the wall of our dutiful duty-full days.

This is a definition of summer that I never managed to give up when I grew up. Hence, though, ariseth my perennially farcical financial situation. Hence my perpetual poker-hand collection of seasonal part-time employments. Hence it is likely I will die with my boots rather than silk slippers on. Hence my and my wife's having chosen to live where there is less job opportunity but more of the kind of countryside that others with more job opportunities consider fine vacation spots. Hence my family's vowing to always and evermore partake in nothing less than absolutely ass-kicking summers.

And hence we begin each of those "summers" with a float into the wilds of the San Juan River, southeastern Utah, the Colorado Plateau.

Praise the Gorge!

I bring up these things – these "hences" to go with how Sarah and I have chosen to live the supposedly "mature" years of our lives – because this is how it's been for twenty years now. And for that, I have to thank the other companion with me on this river trip: Edward Abbey, in the form of a galley-proof of his soon-to-be-released collected letters, *Postcards from Ed*. I brought this along ostensibly because I'm to write a review of the book; I am finding, though, that this new stash of Abbey's writing is also making me review the life-story that I myself have written – in actions – over the last twenty years.

I keep bringing up "the last twenty years," by the way, because it was exactly twenty years ago this weekend that my and Sarah's paths first crossed (then entwined, then entangled). Two decades ago we were both ski bums in the same northern Colorado mountain valley. When we met, it was already ski-bum "summer": I was between seasonal jobs, and was cashing in the fringe benefits of unemployment in the mountains: fishing daily to eat, and toasting those fresh Rocky Mountain trout entrees with pocket-change purchases of Schaefer beer ($1.50 a six pack).

But work was on the horizon. I'd begun spending those high-country mud-season days training to become a river guide. Every morning our little assembly of trainees and instructors would gather to assault various chilly, thumping stretches of whitewater – the Colorado, Blue, and Arkansas rivers – where in trial-by-paddle fashion we learned to read the river; and when we didn't read so good, to high-side, swim rapids, unwrap boats from boulders, and rescue other involuntary swimmers and their crafts from the many hazards of raging snowmelt.

I quickly knew – that bodily awareness and sensual sensibility thing – that I had found my place.

When I first saw Sarah, I was finishing one of those trout dinners on the front porch of the old post office building I was living in. Sarah pulled up driving a roofless Jeep CJ-7 with chrome wheels and a keg strapped into the back seat like a rotund friend. Sarah was the roommate of a fellow river-guide trainee, and she was stopping by to deliver an invitation to my friend's birthday bash. I accepted promptly: I set down my plate, quaffed my Schaefer, jumped the five steps from porch to roadside and into the idling Jeep, which, she has told me often since, was not what she had in mind. No matter: I didn't get out of that Jeep until she sold it three years and 20,000 miles later.

Sarah soon joined our guiding crew. And so began the hences of our life together.

I was doing this, by the way – this learning to run rivers, yes, but also the ski bumming, the inhabiting little mountain hamlets, the (mostly) voluntary poverty, the fishing a lot, the roaming the West, the country, the world, etc. – in no small part due to the influence of Edward Abbey. His books, I mean; I never actually met the man. But that was quite powerful enough.

Three years before meeting Sarah I had migrated West as a sort of back-road detour from the trip-tic route in life I'd been navigating – academic to professional to homeowner to family to beer gut to loss of body pigment to mid-life muscular attrition to pension retirement to hip-replacement surgery and, then, if not sooner, unto death. Or something like that. Or so it seemed. Or so it would've gone if I hadn't stalled out somewhere between the "academic" and "professional" segments of my journey. Fortunately. Hence, a friend-motivated diversion West for a season with the aim of refocusing enough so I could get back onto the mass-cultural interstate.

Fortunately, again, my aim was poor. For it wasn't long after my first purifying, hypnotizing, baptismal Rocky Mountain snowfall that I stumbled onto *Desert Solitaire*, Abbey's rhapsodic, poetic, philosophic treatise on living in a landscape. Which turned out to be just the appetizer, for I quickly acquired an appetite, and soon devoured Ed Abbey's books – *Down the River, Abbey's Road, Beyond the Wall, The Monkey Wrench Gang, Black Sun, The Brave Cowboy,* and *Fire on the Mountain* – like the fat guy at a pig roast.

Hence ...

Back in the early '80's, soon after I came West and before I met Sarah, my mountain-town girlfriend of the time and I decided to write Edward Abbey a letter telling him just how much we'd been inspired by his words. (Meaning: we were living cheap, exploring much, and speaking out loudly about the waste, stupidity, and greed we could already see devouring the West, like we'd seen it gnaw away at the East.) We didn't expect much – by then, Abbey already was a larger-than-life legend, and we figured he had better things to do than respond to groupie fan letters.

We were amazed, then, when, less than a week later, an index-card reply arrived in our little mountain-town mailbox with the return address of "Oracle, Ariz."

"Dear Pam," the handwritten salutation said, followed by, "Thank you for your kind and generous words ... "

The rest of the card was filled with words I don't remember – following our breakup, my former love wasn't about to hand over that prize ("It's addressed to *me*," she reminded me) – but it wasn't meaningless drivel. In the space available, Abbey had responded to and discussed our letter, thoughtfully and sincerely.

And at the end was that signature: Ed Abbey.

It's an event that has stuck with me. That prompt, sincere, and personal postcard from Ed I took as tangible evidence of the character of a man who otherwise was merely mythic to me, affirming my initial sense of someone who put his convictions into action. A small act, but it was, I believe, a manifestation of his personal philosophy of both honor and action. It was his own way of living out that philosophy.

Abbey himself in a letter to an interviewer probably best describes the underlying stream of consciousness running through all his work: "What I am writing about, what I have always written about, is the idea of human freedom, human community, the real world which makes both possible, and the new technocratic industrial state which threatens the existence of all three."

Or, more concisely, perhaps: "If my books have a common theme, it would be something like human freedom in an industrial society" – a concept to which he appended elsewhere: "The conflict is ancient; only the technology has been improved." These statements, in my mind, best represent the least-understood aspect of Edward Abbey's writings. For those with a cursory sense of his work, he is perhaps most recognized as the author of *The Monkey Wrench Gang*, his ribald comedy about a very serious topic: the sabotage – for which he coined the term "monkey wrenching" – of the machinery of development in defense of the land.

But I think it's somewhat unfortunate that he is best remembered for this book, as delightful and fun and funny and provocative as it is. Because it seems to me that when Abbey's work is taken as a whole, a deeper, more powerful, more meaningful, more valuable – and, for most of us radical folks disinclined to the Molotov-cocktail approach to improving the world – more applicable yet no less revolutionary path to action, to fighting in that "ancient conflict," reveals itself.

"Heroes?" Abbey once wrote, answering a friend's query, "I've known a few. People who do good, useful work, who succeed in raising a couple of decent children, who can stay in one place and become citizens of a working community."

This, to me, is the real radicalism of Edward Abbey: Where you are is who you are. That the latter depends on the former. That this yin-yang dance of geography and living well – an unavoidable reality encoded in our human genome – is also action. Also, though, he pointed out that in the world we live in today, the defense and survival of the former – the earth we stand on – depends upon the integrity and courage of the latter, of how we do our living.

We must fight – yes – and Abbey made that point sword-sharp; but, he also entreated us all to remember to live good lives. To remember *how* to live good lives. To *live.* To live *well.* Where we are. How we are. However things are. And not just for ourselves: but for our kids, and their kids, and for the earth that sustains us all now and then – for all those it is vital we remember to live well. That we study those skills, remember those skills, practice those skills, teach those skills, and pass those skills on.

This, too, is monkey wrenching.

This is the story woven through the writings of Edward Abbey. It's an ancient message – Abbey didn't invent it – and Abbey's writings were just another way of articulating what is ultimately a sense, a sensibility, for which there is and can be no One Way, for which there is only each's way. But, Abbey's writings argue, there is nonetheless a right way: if how one lives works to strengthen life, land, our unique individual senses of self, and the well-being of our families and communities.

For isn't that ultimately what we ache for? For meaningful and valuable things to do – skills and tasks and challenges that test and better ourselves? To find a place, a landscape, to love and to know and on which to write our own story? To get to know ourselves and manifest our personal styles of being, to be who we cannot not be? And for some symbiotic, synergistic bonding with others, forging greater wholes to devote ourselves to and of which we can each know we play a part?

Aren't those human needs that transcend any historical time, place, or culture? And aren't those the very things our present way of living – our mass culture of growth and development and marketing and coercion and accumulation of material wealth and power – devours?

I think so. And I think that's what Abbey was saying.

～

Needless to say, Abbey was, in a way, my literary life coach for a while, my anti-career counselor when I needed it most. Thanks to

Abbey and the places his books sent me – philosophical as well as geographic – I never got back on that long and winding downhill road to economic success and domestic rigor mortis I'd begun to run in the city back East. And I bow to Ed Abbey for offering me that view of the topography off that map.

Hence, I walked away, even if I didn't wander so far away. Sure, I've still ended up with a home, a family, jobs, friends and neighbors. Yes. Absolutely. But those very things have become my own personal paths to action. I've learned that the mundane matters. Also, now, though, whilst en route to those things, I also wander the country-side around me that until I came West had remained only a scenic backdrop in my life, like the blur passing by my career-careening car's windshield.

Hence ….

Sarah and I continued to ski bum and river guide and travel for years after that first meeting. Somewhere along the way we got married. Then we settled in a little town on the edge of the Colorado Plateau ("Abbey Country," as he himself shamelessly claimed it). Then we had two kids whom we now raise in this place, running rivers, skiing, hiking, biking, exploring, sleeping out a lot. And we share all this with a band of companions and campeñeros who have made the same choices of how and where and with whom to travel their lives. And who salute all that by starting each summer with a float down the San Juan River.

Hence, twenty years later, I am monkey wrenching by parenting.

Our third day on the river, we are camped at Ross Rapid. Here the river is embedded in a narrow, steep, stair-stepping corridor of grey and golden bedrock. And here, where the river sweeps to the left, a slotted side-canyon spews in debris from river-right. The result is a big bench for camping; a wide, shallow, gently swirling eddy for playing; and a constricting of the river itself so it bunches into a swift series of standing waves as it passes by our beached boats. A much-favored and traditional campsite on the annual San Juan trip.

Much happens here: For hours, we all paddle and surf the duck-ies in the wave train, and the kids make dozens of life-jacketed plum-mets through the rapid – scrambling upstream, jumping in again, bobbing the waves, then stroking hard to catch the eddy below. Good practice for river-rats-in-training. Later, the baseball gloves come out and some of us whip a ball around the knee-deep eddy's infield. Others wander up onto the limestone benches above camp to garner views over our impromptu village and to pay homage to Kenny Ross, the deceased Bluff, Utah-based river runner for whom this surreal, soulful spot is dedicated. (His sage aphorism, "Recognize, don't memorize!" is emblazoned on a plaque attached to a boulder above the river, and has become our group's defacto motto.)

Still later, as darkness fills the canyon, the cocktail flag will be raised, a red monkey wrench on a black field, my personal pirate flag. A filling river-dinner will be concocted and shared. Then chairs will then be encircled, toasts made, jokes and stories told, guitars brandished and songs sung until the first-quarter moon follows the sun behind the ragged canyon rim. Then, our little band of nomads will fall asleep under the stars.

And I will again pass another night doing just what I most want where I most need to be. Because it's who I most am.

Yes, after this river trip, after the adventures of another summer, we will still confront that ennui and tedium and fatigue of the routine tasks and distractions of daily life, even here in Abbey Country. Yes, there will still be the "hence" of the concerns and challenges of finances and jobs. Yes, I still will be likely to die with my boots on – or river sandals, if I'm lucky. Or barefoot, if I'm truly blessed. Such is price of living differently, of carving the life we want and need – a creative life in a beautiful place with people we care about – that is off our modern world's economic thoroughfare.

But that's okay. Because the mundane matters. It is the clay with which we shape our own culture for our own kinds of lives. And that raw material is right here, right where we live. Right how Sarah and I have chosen to raise our family. Right with these others on this magical, mystical, ancient river who have also chosen to make a stand and write their own story with us in this place.

Right where Abbey said it was.

Doing It

*Life is not in the form
but in the flame.*
E. Graham Howe

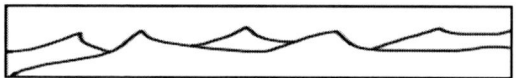

Ode to the San Juan

I used to dream about the San Juan River. Well, day dream, anyway. Day dream while in class at the University of New Hampshire in Hydrology 416, to be exact, because spread across several pages of that course's textbook were long black-and-white aerial photos of a freak of nature: A river inside a uniquely symmetrical canyon – a deep canyon – that, for dozens of miles, snaked in a remarkably close-to-perfect sinusoidal wave pattern.

A sinusoidal wave pattern, for those of you who haven't taken Hydrology 416 ("Streamflow Dynamics"), is the ideal wave form flowing water seeks as it endeavors to meander, because it allows the stream to release the most amount of energy most evenly over the course of the stream. Basically, it's the most efficient path to entropy.

In that way, we are kindred spirits, the San Juan and I.

After college, my own version of a career in the field of hydrology devolved into an impoverished life joyfully passed as ski bum, river rat, and, most recently, backcountry parent. I ended up more of a hydrophile than hydrologist, really – that most efficient path to entropy thing. And, like the San Juan, I endeavored to pursue that path wildly, scenically, and mostly lazily, punctuated here and there with variety and challenge, like the occasional rapid and flash flood found on the San Juan. Mostly lazily, though. Like the San Juan.

And that's why I like the San Juan River.

No, love.

And I say that shamelessly – I am a proud riverhugger. And of the many rivers I've hugged, none means so much to me as the San Juan. As long as I have lived in the Rocky Mountain Southwest – more than a quarter of a century now – the San Juan has meandered through my life, and for the last dozen years or so, through my kids' lives as well, as it runs through the lives of many river lovers here in the Four Corners.

Technically, the stretch of the river I'm referring to is the San Juan's most popular: the 84-mile run in southeastern Utah from Sand Island to Clay Hills, from near the little hamlet of Bluff, to the silt-filled upper arm of Glen Canyon Reservoir (better known by its marketing title, Lake Powell). This desert river run has been made renown by many famous authors – Wallace Stegner, Edward Abbey, Katie Lee, Ellen Meloy, and more – and that advertising has made the river a popular one.

Many of these people, of course, are one-timers – paying customers on commercial river trips. And every year, new private boaters get around to checking it out. But many of these people who run the San Juan each year are repeat visitors – San Juan fans, people who get to the San Juan every year. And some of those – like myself – are true San Juan heads, who find themselves on this river several times each year.

Still it's not a river run for everyone. There is little whitewater to draw the adrenaline-junkie class of river runner. The San Juan is no hairball Cataract Canyon, no challenging Middle Fork, no threatening Arkansas. There are no Lava Falls or Satan's Guts or Snaggletooths to get a boatman's heart pumping or to produce wild tales to tell around the bar back home. And that, right there, is one reason the San Juan River means so much to so many of us: because rather than big water, the San Juan is instead about – dare I say it? – slow, quiet, contemplative, peaceful floating. It's about beauty and boredom. And it's about the unique opportunity to immerse yourself in those rare blessings for days on end, because (especially since the submersion of the stunning and slow-flowing Glen Canyon in the 1960s) the San Juan offers a rare gem: a multi-day, even many-day, remote wilderness flatwater float trip.

By the time it reaches southeastern Utah, the San Juan has already gathered most of its liquid mass, having collected the flows from the southern flank of the San Juan Mountains, where it runs like a gutter gathering such lovely alpine tributaries as the Piedra, Animas, and Mancos rivers. From there, the full-strength San Juan carves itself a path across the gentle high-desert slope of the upper Colorado Plateau.

This may be a gentle slope, but not an easy one. Once past the Sand Island boat launch, the San Juan enters the tortured landscape of bent bedrock that I studied in college from so far afield – layers of sandstone folded into "anticline" upwarps and sediment-filled "syncline" bowls; long, fractured and displaced pieces of earth, like Comb Ridge and Clay Hills; and the eroded remnants of ancient ocean bottoms standing exposed as innumerable and startling monuments and buttes and the great curtainous escarpment of Cedar Mesa.

Upon – and within – this broken and eroded landscape resolutely flows the San Juan, its course etched into and across this terrain in an illogically plotted route. It seems to go the hard way: through the rises of anticlines, across the long draws of synclines, bisecting the gory breaks of the ridges and escarpments. And through it all, the San Juan aspires to meander in wide bow-tie turns, most near-perfectly manifested in the stretch called "The Goosenecks." The San Juan chose this course when the ancient sea had freshly receded, leaving behind a smooth, gentle, exposed ocean bottom that lent itself to the river finding its own dream: those elegantly entropy-seeking sinusoidal waves.

As the Colorado Plateau began to rise, tilting upward on the eastern edge in response to the militant uprising of the San Juan Mountains, the great scouring of the landscape began. But the San Juan held true to its form, to its hydrologic dharma, to its dance with efficient entropy, and just kept slicing its meanders down into the landscape crumbling around it. The result is what we have today: a silty, colorful desert stream set in deep, steep, crumbling sandstone canyons that seem to endlessly bend and twist. And when the river does leave the canyon, it's to cross the great plain of the Mexican Hat Syncline, land of spectacles: Monument Valley and Valley of the Gods and Mexican Hat Rock and the great banded chevrons of the Raplee Anticline. Then, it's back inside its bending bedrock corridor.

To make a really long story really short, my wife and I came along a few million years after the San Juan started its career.

By then I'd begun my own career as a professional hydrophile. I'd been living in northern Colorado, ski bumming in the winter, then following the snowmelt down into the streams as a river guide the rest of the year, until the snows returned. In that role, I'd gotten to explore many of the lovely rivers the region offers, but the San Juan remained a tale – it was a wilderness river in the remote Four Corners area, and none of my river-rat friends cared enough to do the work to visit a river that offered no meaningful whitewater challenges.

It wasn't until my wife and I moved to southwestern Colorado that we finally got to see in person what was inside that textbook of mine many years earlier. In the blistering heat of late summer, Sarah and I loaded gear and food and our dog into a borrowed raft and pushed out for ten days of … well, we really didn't know what we were getting into.

What we got into, though, was a river suited like no other to our own entropic Buddha-natures. We passed those ten days mostly naked and completely surrendered to the slow slide of the San Juan's steady silt-laden current. We sat, and looked around, and rowed some, and sat, and looked around some more. At night, we sat around little driftwood fires that were outshined by those ridiculous, gleaming, laser-like desert stars. Next day, same thing. That's about it. For nearly a week and a half.

Boring for many, I know. I know our big-water buddies we guided with were right to think there was nothing they were looking for here. But Sarah and I also knew that we had found exactly what we were seeking. Nothing.

So much nothing, in fact, we have gone down the San Juan several times a year every year since. Faithfully. Religiously. Reverently.

It's not all boredom, of course. We've had adventures.

There was the time we woke up in the morning to find that the river had risen from 1,000 c.f.s. to 10,000 c.f.s. over night. Our boats were still there, tied high, fortunately. And we were camped up on a bench, luckily. But: Portable toilet: gone. Baseball gloves (standard

San Juan gear): gone. Duckie: gone. River Baby, a plastic doll with hair like Eraserhead that had ridden our bow for years: swum away. A friend's entire dry box: disappeared. (In a remarkable, surreal epilogue, though, this drybox resurfaced hours later and several miles downstream, rising like a submarine and then bobbing merrily directly in front of our friend's boat.)

Another time, a distant rim-top lightning storm kicked up canyon-funneled winds that encrusted our lovely grilled tenderloin dinner with fine San Juan silt. Not a problem – that's part of the luxury desert experience – but when it blew the roll-a-table, complete with table settings, across the beach and began lifting the children off their feet, we decided to retreat to the shelter of our tents. That retreat was halted when I led our kids by flashlight to where I thought our tent was, to find it wasn't. A scan of the area – the kids huddled under a sheltering tamarisk – revealed nothing. A wider search by headlamp began to uncover scattered debris. Slowly, and with no help from the wind, sand, and flashing lightning, the debris – a book, kids' pjs, a couple of sleeping bags – became like breadcrumbs on a trail marking the path of our airborne tent, which we eventually found hundreds of yards away, settled on a shelf up a sidecanyon.

Another trip showed us another side of the San Juan, when a couple of friends and I decided to try an early-season run. We knew the river would be little-visited in early March, so we were excited for the solitude. So much so, that we each took our own, enormous raft, figuring each having his own craft would lead to greater peace, serenity, and independence. What we didn't count on was those lovely early-spring winds that eventually bring those pretty late-spring flowers. Before the flowers, though, those winds howled across the southeastern Utah desertscape, lifting so much of the red sand so high in the sky that the bottom of the clouds glowed a dull rose like sunset at noon, and kicked up muddy standing whitecaps on the reddish river. For three days the three of us inched, literally, with all the effort we could muster, our crafts downstream while the wind pushed the river and everything on it back toward the San Juans, a hundred and fifty miles upstream.

And then there was the other season when I and two other equally determined and deranged friends traveled the river in the middle of an autumn snowstorm, and spent the nights huddled under low overhangs drinking beer and listening to the World Series on a pocket radio. The days, though, were pure sweetness – cold sweetness, but still sweet, as for three days we paddled through the rain and sleet and snow inside the dull grayscale canyon. I finally felt I was inside that black-and-white textbook photograph of the mysterious San Juan I had dreamed about decades before.

Fun stuff, both the adventures and the many, many more hours, days, weeks, and years we have spent just doing that sitting, and looking around, and rowing, and more sitting and looking around that Sarah and I discovered was the soul of the San Juan on our first trip down.

Still, the real value of the San Juan River in our lives didn't become clear until the kids starting joining us.

They started young. Both our kids passed their first week-long trips on the San Juan in playpens strapped over the top of the gear pile in the stern of our cataraft. Sure, they also spend time on our laps, and running around the beaches, and even floating in the warm swirling water, but they mostly were in the playpen just ... you know: sitting and looking around. And napping to the soft slosh of the river on the tubes. After that, they graduated to hanging out on a table we strapped across the bow of our tubes.

The only problem came the first time we hit some particularly big sand waves. Sand waves, it should be noted, are found only on the San Juan River: only the San Juan has the correct combination of slope, sediment texture, and flow volume to create moving wave trains in the river bottom itself, which then produce tall, narrow, curling standing waves on the river's surface. Making them even more bizarre, these sand waves have a life span of only a few minutes – so a line of enormous sand waves can rise, crest and rage for two or three minutes, then shrink back away to flat water, appearing elsewhere a few minutes later.

Our first sand waves with the kids were startling: They rose so fast and steeply that what had been smooth water soon swept our kids off the bow and into the river. The first few times kind of freaked us all out. Soon, though, it became no big deal for all – the kids learned how to enjoy bobbing in the big waves (a good skill to practice), and we learned to just hang near them until the sand waves passed and we could pull them in.

Our kids have matured now, after more than ten years on the

San Juan. Both Anna and Webb have learned to row the raft and paddle a duckie. Webb has even solo paddled Government Rapid, the biggest rapid the San Juan has to offer. And they have, of course, survived adventures: not just the sand waves, but also those winds, the storms, the flash floods, the red ants, the cold spring nights, the hot summer days ... all the things a desert river offers.

Mostly, though, and most importantly, I believe, they have learned to survive – no, not just survive, but to actually enjoy – the boredom. The flatwater. The quiet. The solitude. The just sitting, and looking around, and sitting some more. This, any parent knows, is not easy for kids these days. In a media-saturated world like the one our kids today are growing up in, boredom is anathema, feared, avoided at all costs, presented and perceived as a useless waste of vital energy.

But sometimes, my wife and I believe, entropy is a good thing. Sometimes, in the right place, for the right reasons, boredom is not a wasting of energy at all, but ... an opportunity, an option, a portal. Sometimes, if that just sitting, and looking around, and maybe rowing or swimming or napping, is done over and over in the same magical, mythical place, it can lead to a blending of that energy and that place. An awareness. A sort of landscape literacy, a worldly intimacy. "Hear the murmuring of the stream?" a Taoist master once asked. "There is the way ..."

For Sarah and me, like for many of us San Juan Riverheads, the San Juan is the way to tap that power of entropy. And for the kids, through years of doing that, through growing up down there in those canyons, the San Juan has become their place. Our place. All of our place. The place we go to dream.

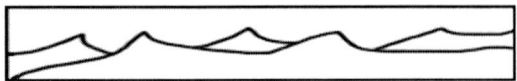

Men's Tripping

"So, you're here for the forty-eight-hour vision quest, is that right?"

Bob busts a laugh. "Yeah, that's right."

We lock the truck, grab our lifejackets, and head down the beach, where we join the others for a quick safety meeting. We want to be sure we're all on the same page. Or river, at least. And we need to be safe, because it is night-time. There's a full moon, true; but it's dimmed considerably by the cloud cover. And It's cold. But none of that's unusual this time of year, it being November and all.

And it's not unusual because this is the Annual San Juan River Men's Canoe Trip. It's like this every year, pretty much, because that's when we go: on the full moon in November. So: Cold is good. Moonlight and midnight are good. Canoes are very good. The river and its canyon ahead are very, very good. And a group of men out for forty eight hours together on a remote autumn river is so very, very good.

I won't try to tenderize our behavior with any deep pseudo-philosophical male-bonding blabber. We're not the drumming-and-loin-cloth type of male-gatherers – that holds about as much allure for me as a sleepover at Michael Jackson's house. No, we're more the meat and beer and paddles and baseball kind o' guys. (That's right: the Annual San Juan River Men's Canoe Trip always involves a full-nine-inning full-bore baseball game (with sandbar rules)). So I may as well get to the point, and state right up front the value, meaning, purpose, drive and spirituality behind the Men's Trip. It is just this: River. Cold. Full moon. Men, being only men, in canoes in the midst of the other three. Just this. There is no deeper reasoning. There's no reasoning at all, for that matter. And that's the point.

Our safety issues settled, we launch. Bob climbs into the front of my happy big red canoe, pushes off from the beach with his right pile-pant-covered leg ("piles o' pile," we call our manly Fall fashion scheme), slips into his seat at the bow, and takes a few deep strokes as I guide us out onto the weakly luminescent river. The other boats glide darkly behind us as the river conveys us into the murky night.

The hours are passed passing a shadowy, ghostly landscape of dim bluffs and tamarisk shadows and the amorphous movement of the water. In the darkness we feel for the flow as much as we seek it by sight. This means sometimes scraping the Royalex over rock bars, and a few times it means having to step out into the chilly river to lighten the load and drag our craft over some unseeable low-water river-bottom rising.

Mostly, though, we float. I settle back and savor it all … the blurry moon, the other-worldly desertscape, the river-carried drift of the boat. Conversation is minimal, unimportant, functional rather than social. Yes, occasionally boats bob in range of each other and some chatting and bantering ensues … then we again find our own stretches of river, float our own psychic flows …

Until my solitary thoughts are interrupted prematurely by an explosion of water from somewhere just out of sight in the darkness.

"Well," a voice echoes across the water, "you gotta have beaver on a men's trip!"

Morning: We stand around the camp, which is set around an enormous cottonwood that has managed to crawl its trunk across the sand, then shoot up a low canopy above the water. The day is cold-air desert clear – a surreal blue sharp behind a ridge of rusted redrock. Coffee is brewed and poured and brewed again.

Each men's trip draws its own unique crew, like an eddy catching flotsam. Scott, Eric, and myself are the truly addicted, the pushers. This year there is also a pleasant mix of repeat offenders and rookies. Dave's and Matt's presence is becoming regular enough to warrant concern. And there are a few new initiates: Bill, who although is new to this particular all-male revue is a familiar enough river rat (best known for his hourly watchman-style reports: "Hot in the desert!"); Dan, whom I don't know yet, but who appears ready to prove his mettle in his brand new, shiny, wedding-present canoe; and Bob. Bob has been a Colorado mountain-town compatriot of mine for the past two decades, but through it all I have not been able to get him out of his mountain hermitage and onto the river. "I'm a mountain man," he'd rationalize, "not a river rat." But I am a true friend. So through a campaign of relentless questioning of his manhood, I finally wore him down and lured him aboard.

Breakfasts come out. Simple stuff: Meat, cheese, granola bars, even the occasional dainty fruit. The flat November sun finally falls across us like the dawning of a bright idea (which is as close as we'll probably get to one). Pile is unpiled. People wander off to move around: A couple go for walks. Some climb the escarpment behind camp. A few even play catch to warm up, chucking the ball across sand and rabbitbrush, training for the upcoming game.

For me and Scott, it's a swim.

This is something of a ritual for the two of us – we are always the only two to swim on the Men's Trip. We strip down on the beach and walk out: first through a stagnant pool, than across a damp sand bar, then into the wide, calf-deep channel. We strut through the water, each endeavoring to be a little cooler than the other by seeming a little warmer, but what I'm really thinking is that it's not very fair. Scott's from Ontario. But I hang with him, dragging my numb legs until we finally find a place to drop and do a quick upstream push up. We rise and casually, calmly, and with great affected poise stroll back to camp to, we are sure, the accolades of our impressed comrades.

We get back to camp to find Bill, Eric and Dan washing down their sausage and eggs, green like fungus with chilies, with cans of beer. Matt and Bob are whipping a baseball at each other. Scott and I stand there (dressed again) all wet and grinning and happy as my kids on a snow day from school.

They look up and study us.

"Did you go swimming?" Eric asks.

And I'm crushed.

Bill laughs. "Cold in the desert!" he bellows.

ln

This is rather how the trip goes, with variation of lovely locale and spiced with doses of action. We all stop to hike around the enormous, weird, alien-looking volcanic remnant called the Mule Ear

Diatreme. Scott and I run – another male bondage ritual we share – an insane, up and down, rock-and-scree sprint, for miles and miles, crisscrossing washes, and finally ascending and descending the great ugly plug. Back on the river we head into the canyon, where we spend hours shifting between floating and staring at the scenery – lovely golden-and-grey banded canyon walls, fractured and spilling debris down to the river – and navigating tight, rocky rapids rearranged from how we remember them by the summer's big floods.

Near dark, our flotilla arrives at Eight Foot, the biggest rapid we'll encounter on our venture – a blind-corner entry into a 75-or-so-yard shot down a fast, bouldery run. Bob and I swing around the rock outcropping with our ferry angle ready, and then paddle hard. Sighting on our line and leaning into my paddle in the back of the boat, I see far downstream a red canoe overturned. As we shoot past the capsized boat, we can see Dan on shore gathering his gear into a pile.

That night we gather around a nice fat fire. For my dinner, I sizzle a slab of beef on an old refrigerator-shelf grill. I complement this with bread and a fresh garden salad (from a bag). The moon is clear, at last. We drink tons more beer. Later: shots. At some point, I scribble by firelight in my little pocket notebook: *Everything in moderation, including moderation.* Much later, Eric introduces a game called "eating box," involving a 12-pack box, balance, and no hands.

Dan gets to go first, to redeem his honor.

"I live by my wife's clock," the batter states, continuing his conversation with his three teammates as he steps up to the plate (a frisbee).

"Yeah, and you're here 'cause it's now half-past can't," taunts the second baseman/shortstop/centerfielder.

It's somewhere near the end of the game, but we're not quite sure. But it doesn't matter: our tin cups runneth over, and my team is down by four runs. Or five. And there have been plenty of Sportscenter-quality plays: diving stops in the sand, a leaping catch off the four-foot section of eroded beach, and a couple of full-sprint over-the-shoulder catches down "home run alley," the sloping stretch of sand between the tamarisk wall and the river, which are both automatic outs.

We have to head out tonight, but that's still many hours away, so we play on. But already I can feel something … like déjà vu …

A few weeks before the Men's Trip, I chaperoned on my daughter's class field trip. It was to a local nature-center's property along a little nearby river. Buff, crumbly sandstone bluffs surround the sparse pinion-juniper forest along the river, through which the staff and volunteers have cut interpretive trails. It's a great place to bring kids to wander and explore.

My duty was to ride herd on the small group of boys. And I understood why: they were fidgety, unattentive and impolite when the naturalist would stop to explain some interesting point about the ecology and Nature. I tried patience. Then firmness. Even scolding, until I realized that even I could no longer maintain enthusiasm and focus for the explanations and demonstrations.

It all reached a climax at the riverside, when our guide was pointing vaguely into the stream, outlining the life that lived somewhere under that surface. I covertly led my five charges downstream, and proceeded to teach them how to catch crayfish by standing in the water and looking under rocks. For the next half hour, they were focused, interested, questioning, learning, and applying what they learned. They were seeing firsthand what was below the surface of the river.

At one point, I heard one of the boys behind me say excitedly to another, "This is the best thing I've ever done!"

When it was time to go, we had to drag the boys away from the river, wet feet and all.

I feel I'm going to have to be dragged away from the river. Or carried.

And I know I'm not alone. Bob's hooked. I could tell by the way he ate box last night.

Dave drives the ball to his taunting opponent, who throws him out at first base (my lifejacket). Third out. The other team comes in to take their hacks.

"What inning is it, anyway?" Dave asks.

"No matter what inning it is," Bob says from somewhere off to the side, "always live like it's the bottom of the last." We all look. He smiles shyly and drains his cup.

"Hey!" I exclaim. "I think Bob's forty-eight-hour vision quest worked!"

It must be the seventh inning stretch, because no one heads to the field; instead we huddle around the bow of Bill's boat to pass snacks – jerked meat, gorp, and canned oysters on crackers. And we refill our mugs. Everything in moderation.

Eric speaks up. "That's what I hate about this trip," he whines, "same shit every year."

"Right," says Bill. "Next year, just meat and beer."

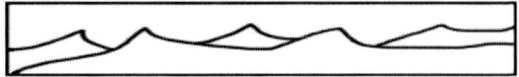

Doing It

*M*y wife remembers her first time.

She was on her family's annual ski trip. She had been skiing all her life, and every year her parents made sure their family got away to the mountains, some mountains somewhere, to ski for a week together. (And they still do, even now with grandkids.)

She was fourteen that year, the year their trip was to Taos, New Mexico. One afternoon, a few days into the trip, everyone else had gone in already, but she decided to stay out, by herself, to get in a few more runs. It was late afternoon, and March's flat sun had already fallen behind the headwall of Taos' famed double-blacks, leaving the runs blue. She was riding a lift alone up the face of the mountain when it came to her:

I want to be able to do this all the time.

It took a while, but that was it, really. She went back to Illinois and finished high school, then rolled on through college. After graduation, she and a friend threw their stuff into the back of a convertible and rolled West. A year later, she met me – a couple of years earlier I had thrown some gear in the back of a friend's van and headed West.

Since then we've always lived somewhere where we can do it a lot.

On a June morning, Bob and I do it.

We start out in the grey predawn toward a great banded peak ahead of and above us. Bob and I have been skiing together since I first arrived out here. Bob ended up in the Rockies by running out of money in Colorado during a long bicycle trip. We met while we were both driving mountain-town buses through great night-time blizzards (this was the early 1980s in northern Colorado, when great blizzards were the order of the day), and spending our days playing on, in, around, and through – on particularly munificent powder days – the manna those storms left behind.

Two decades later, we're still in the same state, and states of mind. We live in another corner of Colorado, but we still live very near great, glorious mountains, and the snow they gather and offer.

Today's offering is corn. It is very-late spring, after all. And we love corn. So we share a bowl of it, so to speak, heading toward a big north-facing basin hanging between the many faces of the big peak and a lower, no-less-menacing tower. The basin harbors the stems and seeds of winter's stash, and we aim to partake.

I take the high road, angling along the top of the snow line as it parallels the base of the most radical drop off the top of the ridge. Bob takes the low road up the center of the basin. We have no problem with each going his own way; it's the way we've always done it. We reconvene high in the middlest of the middle of the snowfield. We snack. We look around. We smell and feel the damp air on our shirtless skin and feel the corn snow rolling though our chilled fingers. Someone points somewhere and talks about what he sees – a distant river gorge … a high-desert mountain range … a town … a rolling hill … an idea.

Our reverie is broken by thunder – the sound of summer coming – drumming from over the ridge behind us. Flags from the storm's advancing front line already fly overhead, from over the ridge, from over the unseen peaks behind us.

So we do it.

My moment had nothing to do with skiing. It had to do with driving.

I was headed out of Boston on the main-artery urban-exodus death-drive known as Route 2, the same route down which those "terrorist" Colonialists chased – guerilla-style, "Indian"-style, insurgent-style – the retreating Red Coats after the Battle of Lexington and Concord. Today that route is still essentially that same meandering "cart road," just paved over.

I had graduated from college the year before, and was working in the city making good money writing software manuals for banking programs. The future looked as bright as a fluorescent light. I drove a 1975 Toyota Wagon – not exactly an urban assault vehicle, but in Boston I had to treat it as such. On the loopy, winding, rotary-wound streets of greater metro Boston – a habitat that surpassed its optimal human population three hundred years ago – offensive driving is defensive driving.

I wanted to get home, so I was driving particularly offensively this Friday afternoon. I was afflicted with that modern American worker's Pavlovian drooling – TGIF ... got to get out of the city ... want to be doing something, anything, anywhere else – me and a half-million other commuters headed to the bedroom towns ringing the city like fancy shanty towns. I was working the Toyota's four little cylinders hard, when, confronting a stationary queue of traffic, I, for some reason I still have yet to come to peace with, opted to not slow down and instead ran the little green car down the median at 50 miles an hour.

I stopped 2,000 miles later.

First there was a short stop at home. I accepted a friend's standing offer to head West with him in his old van. I courteously gave notice at my job. I tried to explain it to my parents. I told my girlfriend I had to go and she could have the new sofa. I assured her I would be back, and probably meant it.

I had to do it.

It's a 30-inch Glory Day at Purgatory, or little local ski area. What timing: my old college roommate is visiting from San Diego. And he is in raw awe – for him, it's like a day of 20-foot swells back home. We ski to exhaustion, on every run. We save any conversation, although little is necessary, for the chairlift.

Great stories will come from this day, we agree. But the best story of the day comes from my friend Matthew when we run into him over on Lift 8. He explains, in the tone of incredulous reverence of someone who has seen the image of Jesus in the head of his beer, that on the way up that morning, driving alone and anxiously anticipating a first-chair big-powder day, he found a freshly car-killed elk on the side of the road. He gutted the elk, threw it in the car, then went and caught the powder day, just a little behind his first-chair ambitions.

That night, Matthew comes over and we share fresh-elk fondue with our wives and friends. My college buddy deep fries his skewered hunk of Southwestern Colorado powder-day road-kill wapiti while on the cell phone giving his wife a play-by-play.

If that ain't it, I don't know what it is.

There was another significant day of skiing with Matthew. Matthew, it's worth mentioning, is the best skier I know personally. "Just a hobby," he says casually – for money, he sues the government for violating its own environmental laws. In my mind, though, that is a noble and worthwhile hobby. Skiing *matters*.

This wasn't just any day, though. It wasn't even just any other powder day: This was My Greatest Powder Day Ever – although I will grant that "greatest ever" powder days are, like sex, circumstantial and never the "ever." And also like sex, it wasn't that it was such a big or deep powder day, it was the style of this day. The snow was just deep enough … and it's flesh was just light enough … it was like the coordinates of those two variables were intersecting into a single, glorious, point – a frozen "GEE!"-spot – that we arrived just in time to catch.

Generally, lift-rides are pragmatic affairs – the foreplay that must be endured in order to get to the huffing-and-puffing workout you're there for. But days like this are different. That first-chair ride up on a powder day is in and of itself a wonderfully, almost painfully, slow, deliberate, invigorating, sensuous experience. You know what's coming so surely, so tangibly, that you don't just desperately crave to get there, you ache to be there now. But … you can't.

You must go through the steps. And you don't mind, because on that first chair you know that smooth, silken bare slope ahead will wait for you and your first touch. So, you be here now. You savor the anticipation. You keep your eyes open – all your senses awake – drinking in the sights on the way to your alpine gratification. And that chair ride becomes its own delightful, intimate, physical experience.

And then, you do it. And it's like no other time you've done it.

Until the next time.

And that day, we did it until we were too tired to do it any more.

$\backsim$

This year my wife's family's ski trip is to Steamboat, in northern Colorado. Sarah's dad, Frank, is now 70 years old and still going strong, still double-pole jump-turning down the spring-soft bumps like he's still on 225 cm hickory sticks. And while doing it, he still yodels in joy.

And I'm experiencing my own joy. And not just from the spring skiing. Here's what I'm yodeling about:

Sarah and I spend the morning with our kids, Webb and Anna, and Sarah's parents, and an assortment of her family members, their kids and some of their friends. It's a powder day – not big, but big enough. We spend the first hour in a pack, three generations together carving turns, sliding hockey stops, and bumping moguls and (mostly the third generation) catching air. After every run we shuffle the deck riding the chair, talking to different people each time.

Mid-morning, Anna and Webb take off – Anna with her teenage cousin and her cousin's girlfriends, and Webb with his cousins – each armed with only a ski-area map. Gone. For hours. To see what they can find on this big mountain they've never skied before. To see where they end up before meeting later at the mountain-top restaurant.

While the kids are gone, Sarah and I ride a chair alone and talk about our nervous excitement about this rite of passage – our kids claiming the mountain as their own. In a way, it's the start of their ski-bum careers. Then, rather like imagining our kids getting their driver's licenses, we think back on our own years in those careers and can't help but wince at what's probably coming: those crazy, risk-taking teen years. Then Sarah sums it up: "I'd rather have my kids here for spring break than Fort Lauderdale or Cancun. There, it's just about getting buzzed and cruising. Here, they'd at least also be getting outside and working at a skill and seeing a beautiful place."

When the kids meet with us later, we hear their stories over cheeseburgers: How, as the mountain got skied off, they knew where to find powder stashes … how they followed the sun and shadows to find the best snow … how Webb got separated from his cousins, so decided to explore a few runs on his own before figuring out his way back to the meeting place …

But my proudest moment came later, when Sarah, Webb, Anna, and I were riding a chair from the restaurant back to the top of the mountain. Below us we witnessed the classic ski-area lift-ride show: a pastel-colored vacationer auguring into the snow at an excessive rate of speed, spewing expensive ski gear into an expansive debris field.

We all watch this show unfold in silence, until Anna says, "Wow, that guy yard-saled!"

And I knew we were passing it on.

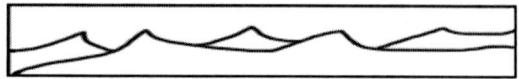

Powder Day

I really had planned on growing up some day. Oh, well.
Instead, here I am, in the middlest of my midlife, standing in a mostly empty parking lot at Purgatory on a weekday morning, pulling on my ski boots. I'm supposed to be working. But it's a powder day. Oh, well.

I had asked my kids if they wanted to skip school and join me today. They both said no, that they had important things to do at school. They're growing up, it seems. I've really got to work on that. I've tried lately. Just a few weeks ago we were staying for a few nights at a condo in some nice resort in a warmer climate. Not really my kind of camping, so, as usual, I quickly got antsy. I needed to get out and play – this resort thing was a bit grown-up for me, it seemed. I wanted to bring my son along, get him out of the box for a while. It took some work: I had to do something somewhere between persuading and dragging to get him out with his skateboard to ride the very cool sidewalks threaded through the manicured landscaping. He was worried about the "No Skateboarding" signs.

"You've got to learn to break some rules," I told him, fatherly. Lovingly. Concerned. Bestowing my great Elder wisdom.

So we struck a deal: If I would bring our dog – there were also signs declaring "No Pets" – then he'd ride his skateboard. We ended up having a great time out roaming around, dodging staff and other guests, exploring that alien world.

I want to be a role model for my kids. I'm working on that, too.

Next to me in the parking lot is a college-age kid, probably also MIA from classes, lacing his snowboard boots on the tailgate of his Jeep. I'm blaring hip hop; he's cranking Ozzie's "Crazy Train" – like we're having a great time roaming around each other's generation.

We nod at each other, grinning, our heads bobbing to our respective beats.

I won't be growing up today.

Soon, though, I am heading up. I have the seat all to myself on the big six-person chairlift rising from the base lodge. When I left town, it was under assault by a wet, driving sleet, splattering into a thick accumulation of slush. The air was dense, damp and chilling. Trees were frosted. The foothill foreground around Durango was reduced to the hogback ridge west of town and the ramp-like silhouette of Animas City Mountain – the hills and mountains behind those had been swallowed. On the highway headed north out of town, the "chains required on passes" sign flashed.

Up here, the aspen ridges reach into the clouds, solid and pulsating like a coastal fog. We're above the freezing-rain level, so heavy, wet snow droops the spruces. The chair soon passes into the cloudbank, and a sloppy snow quickly coats me. I'm eating road-kill elk jerky, swinging my skis and sucking up the spring snowfall. I realize I should get philosophical about this here – that would be the "grown up" thing to do, to rationalize why I've chosen to ditch work on a weekday and play – but … It's a powder day, and I'm just really, really happy. That's it – no deeper thoughts.

Off the lift, I find few other tracks slice the hilltop of new snow. As I skate the flat past the mountain-top patrol hut, a snow slide ejects off the roof. And then, from the top of the Paradise run is a view of paradise … or there should be. Normally from here there is a dazzling view of the distant, enormous, looming fangs of the Needle Range. Today, though, that wall of rock is hidden behind the mass of moisture we passed through on the lift ride up here. But … it's there. I can feel it, that landscape out there. I give it a bow anyway.

I push off and sink into deep telemark turns. The untracked, fresh snow is like a long reach of glassy lake sloped on a thirty degree angle. The mountain and I do a gravity-dance in the pure uncut snowfall on the wide, open run below me. My knee carves the snow like the bow of a boat; behind me my skis leave a wake, reeling out a line of river-meander-like S-turns down the mountain. I pass copses of snow-heavy trees. I dive down the steep pitches marking the limestone ridges the band the mountain. I swing and dip and swing and dip …

Paradise.

Now time for some Pandemonium.

I cut left and under a dormant chairlift. Over the crest of a sharp fall line – like scouting the lip of a nasty rapid from the river – I see a steep field of snow-covered Volkswagen Beetles. Or so it seems. I stop, catch my breath, sniff the air (damp, like a cold spring day), and study potential lines through the boulderfield of moguls that give Pandemonium its name.

Two snowboarders skid to a stop next to me, kicking up an explosion of snow.

"Ya! That was bitching, dude!" one yells, panting, to the other.

Snowboarding seems lovely, and a bunch of my friends do it. My only real concern is that it allows people of very little experience or skill to go very, very fast. The reason I personally don't do it , though – for I still, even at my age, understand the allure of going very, very fast with very little experience or skill – is because it seems going very fast makes the runs down the mountain – which is what I'm here for, after all – go by much too quickly.

But even if I don't get it, these young bucks riding their boards are still part of the Powder Day Tribe. So I bow to them, too.

I then jump into the first turn, and immediately lurch, then lunge, then launch forward, downward, displaying very little of the great amount of skill and experience I have on my telemark skis, and auger my face into a particularly large mogul.

I glide to stop when I have traveled far enough to accumulate in front of me an adequate mass of snow to counteract the downward force of the mass of my body multiplied by the square of my velocity. It takes about 30 yards, it appears, as I look back up at my snowplowing skidmark. I noticed the dude and his buddy are gone – their nearly-straight tracks head past me and over the next rise. I lie there, savoring the cold chill of the snow blown into the tiny weak points of my ski clothing, feel the glow of the flow of blood in my downward-pointing head, and ponder the Zen powder-day lesson in this: Egolessness, Grasshopper.

After that rest, the rest of the run goes better. The hundreds of yards down to the base are filled with fat, happy jump-turns off enormous, clean, fluffy bumps.

The rest of the day is equally filled with fun runs and lovely lift rides. One time, I ski up to an empty lift line and find three snowboarders lying on the snow. Just lying there, exhausted. At the top of a lift, I see two old people merrily poling away; one is wearing one those pile jester hats and the other is in a hat like lizard. On a particularly ridiculously delicious run down Deadspike, I am passed by a guy carving wide, fast, swooshing turns, cheerily singing a Christmas carol: "I hear sleigh bells ringin' ... "

I also get on chairs with a few other people skipping work for this powder day. Like Linda, who I learn is also a telemarker and backcountry skier. We both know this, our home mountain, intimately, so we talk about where to go as the runs get skied off and the snow warms.

Most of the time, though, there are absolutely no lines, so I ride the lifts alone. On lift 5, I observe a reverent moment of silence (which was easy, being alone, of course) as I pass over the site of my friend Matt's recent injury, which has ended his ski season – a small cliff forever henceforth to be known as the Tibial Plateau. On Lift 8, my fatigued body enjoys the slow ride up. I hear hoots and yeehaws coming from the glades of Paul's Park.

By midday, I'm down to stalking the edge lines for powder stashes. Then, the snowfall stops and it grows warm, and suddenly the snow is like mashed potatoes served on a bed of ice. Time to head home – I have to pick up my kids from school, anyway. (Even though they should be up here! Gotta' work on that ...)

I work my way back to the parking lot a little after noon. I'm wet, tired, sore, and behind on my work. But I still think truancy can be a good thing. I may not have grown up today, but at least I've kept up my hooky skills. For when I need it. For when the day deserves it.

And I'm not alone. Walking back through the parking lot, I pass a woman talking to her little kid. "Emma, come get your skis," she pleads. But Emma is walking in her pink snowsuit and little ski boots with her hands outstretched like a zombie, toward a huge snowbank left over from the morning's plowing.

Seemed like she's having a hard time growing up, too.

I get it.

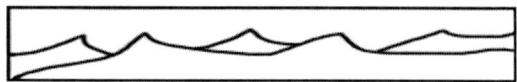

Bumism
(for Dolores)

Y ou know the bum. Ski bum, surf bum, river rat. Island bum, fishing bum, bar fly. Wandering walker, backroads roamer, and neighborhood-savoring front-porch bum.

When we think of bums, we think of those somehow odd, somewhat indolent, often impoverished and generally unproductive people that are found loitering around the places we often like to visit: the ocean, the mountains, the deserts, the funky little nook-and-cranny towns scattered about out in the hinterlands. They come in both male and female, and their ages can run from 18 to 80. (Silverton, Colorado's Dolores LaChapelle, author, Tai Chi master, and the patron saint of powder skiing, recently passed at 82 – still every bit the ski bum as any college-dodging late-teen lift-op.)

Laggards all of them. But they might know something you don't.

Look again: What binds bums of all configurations and in all locations? It is having opted to focus their attention less on making a good living and more on the good living itself. They might have chosen to not be worldly, but they are nonetheless active and involved in their immediate world, where ever that is.

That logic, of course, is a bit circular for the square hole inhabited by the mass of "normal" adults in our present urban/suburban corporate/career producer/consumer culture – hence that image of laziness and frivolity associated with bums. And by most folks' standards, they're right. Bums are loafers. Proudly so. Deliberately so.

Hence, most bums' careers begin as travelers. At some point, each proto-bum hits the figurative and literal road, driven out by what they perceive as the over-mediated and mundane mediocrity of the median modern lifestyle. And they're right, too, by the traveler's figuring of things.

Traveling, of course, is at the heart of the bum. I mean "traveling" as opposed to mere tourism. The true traveler goes to places seeking authenticity, tangibleness, challenge and spontaneous beauty rather than comfort, convenience, ease, and itinerary. And they're willing to put in the time it takes to reach those deeper places hidden inside mere locations. A traveler is someone who heads out into the world – be it wilderness backcountry or urban frontcountry – deliberately, consciously, and conscientiously, to be in a place rather than just to see a place, and to meet the inhabitants as they are rather than watching them perform like on some TV reality show.

That's the traveler. And it's a good life, for a while. But after a while, even a traveler is called to venture into that human wilderness: family, community, and places of their own to become inhabitants of. These are ancient, primordial, irresistible travels, too. But they're places the road doesn't go. They're only found by standing still.

A bum, then, is a traveler who has settled down. Sort of. Not "settled" in the sense most people live it – like the settling of concrete at the base of a dam – but more "settled" in the sense of having settled on a permanent base-camp from which to practice one's traveling. And "down" more in the sense of having traded the wide-breadth of road-traveling for a depth of home-traveling – to turn those traveler's talents and skills and curiosities about the world inward, to the "nearby faraway," as author and hunting bum David Petersen calls the world right around us that we are too often too distracted and too numbed by routine to see.

To really see – as a traveler sees the world, with that traveler's style and spirit and sensibility. But at home. That's the bum.

And that's why bums have made the mysterious choice – mysterious to those on the school/work/career/investment/retirement-fund adventure in life – to settle in some remote town where they struggle to get by, so they can regularly, ritually, and religiously pursue their unprofitable passion or passions of choice – skiing, surfing, paddling, casting, hiking, biking, walking, wandering, sitting and staring at the prettiness all around, or any other number of means of getting out of the indoors and into the great big real "real world" out there. And so they can hang out among a community of others who share the peculiar priorities and those unprofitable, uncivilized, and illogical proclivities that get them labeled "bums" in the first place.

Look again: That's the unique art of the bum – let's call it Bumism: to transform traveling into a lifestyle. Not "lifestyle" like that one we work so hard to earn and build, but lifestyle as life with style. Because if the ultimate wisdom is to know that, regardless of our big ideas and plans, life really only exists in the flash of the moment – "Where ever you go, there you are" – then the bum has turned that into action, reminding us that the real trick is to remember that our life is really only the living itself.

Where ever you are, there you *go*.

That's what the bum knows.

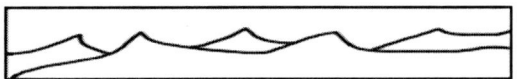

A Skeptic's Pilgrimage to Powell

> *Nobody goes there anymore*
> *because it's too crowded.*
> Yogi Berra

I am unmoved.

Oh, it was a generous gesture, a friend offering to take me out onto Lake Powell for a day. She knew my disparaging feelings on this body of water, despite my otherwise water-loving ways, so she challenged me to come see what Glen Canyon had become after being flooded, rather than continually moaning over what it had once been.

So that's how I got here, on this lovely and cold wintery day, sitting on this spit of sand pushed out into the lakewater by the wide wash to my right. And around me is what my friend had promised: The still-remaining sandstone bluffs and walls and mounds and endlessly diverging canyons of the greater Glen Canyon area above waterline. And it was, as so excites my friend, remarkably easy to reach this place, which at one time would've taken a week or weeks of floating and walking to access.

But I am unmoved.

Still, I want to honor my friend's gift of this day, so I sit here and take in the redrock views. I endeavor to appreciate being here, despite the barrier of my bitter biases. I remind myself that I am deeper than I have ever been, geographically speaking, into the heart of my personal heartland, the Colorado Plateau.

And it has been, as she had assured me it would be, lovely and dramatic. Our 80-mile, several-hour boat ride out here from the marina in Page, Arizona, was as curious as it was glorious, surreal as it was real. We cruised wide expanses of open water encircled by low bluffs and tall buttes. We swept across the hem of the deeply-crevassed bedrock skirt of Navajo Mountain. We shot across near the top of the Crossing of the Fathers, and flew past the steep notch of the hand-chiseled Mormon Trail. We floated over the submerged bedrock ballroom of The Cathedral in the Desert, and bobbed up to once-inaccessible ancient pueblo remains.

Yet even here, even among these mythic and powerful landmarks, I just ain't feeling that redrock love. And it's not because of where I am, but because of how I got here. It's because of what getting here that way says: That no matter how much leftover prettiness there is here above Lake Powell, this is what Glen Canyon and hundreds of miles of its side canyons have become: paved.

I don't mean that as mere metaphor or analogy. Yes, the pavement in this case is water, but that doesn't change the essential fact: What Glen Canyon has become is a major highway system piercing what had not very long ago been some of the most remote, yet accessible, wild country in the continental U.S. Now it is just another big road for those who can afford the big machines now required to journey here. Yet another weekend getaway for the bettering of the motorized recreation industry, and its remotest treasures cheapened into so many more mere roadside attractions. (On this day we traveled in a $50,000, 360 h.p., 18-foot powerboat – which was the smallest craft we saw all day. More common were houseboats by the dozens, even here in the "off season," many pulling behind them ski boats and jet skis, like RVs hauling jeeps and motorcycles.)

I must here admit, of course, that I never actually experienced Glen Canyon before Lake Powell. I arrived in the West after that battle was lost and the invasion complete. And I will also admit, after a day out here with my friend that I have come to appreciate and respect her affection and caring for this place, so full of meaning and pleasure for her. Even if it is Lake Powell.

But today has also shown me that regardless of either of those things, I remain unmoved.

And today has made me realize that it's not because I can't get over it, but because I don't want to get over it.

I don't want to get over it because somebody must remember. Somebody must remember not just what was, but why what's still left elsewhere should stay wild and remote. Because when everything becomes like everything else, when everything is paved and accessed and marketed, we lose options of how to live, how to be, of where to be.

And somebody must remember what could be again: Remote, wild, mythic, sacred spaces for those willing to make – and not just those who can afford – the journey required to get there.

Places to be moved by, and not just move around in.

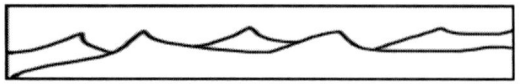

Days of Last Resort:
An unpopular story about some popular notions

We have confused money with wealth.
Alan Watts

*A*t last, winter has come home.

So this morning, with the mountains grinning with a gleaming layer of fresh snow – and this on top of our recent gift of the lately-elusive stuff – my family and I grab our clothes and boots and skis, load the car, and venture north, to the mountains. And to our favorite mal-named but much-loved rinky-dink ski area.

We head north, along with a thin but steady stream of skis and snowboards strapped to roof tops, up the Animas Valley – past the redrock bands like welts on the valleyside's fresh skin of snow, then along the base of the morning-lit aurora-like curtain of the Hermosa Cliffs, to the whitewashed spruce-and-aspen glades at the base of Durango Mountain Resort. Which none of us calls it, since that particularly malevolent marketing moniker balls up like peanut butter on the tongue. How about "DMR"? Ack. So we still just call it Purgatory. Or "Purg" – as ski bums have called it for forty years – when even that's too much, too formal, too impersonal, too unfriendly for the deep, warm familiarity we feel for this place. Especially on a grand powder day such as we have before us here today.

Parking is easy – we four-wheel our way into one of the snowy lots near the bottom runs. Soon, we've geared up, walked over, and loaded onto the short lift up to the main base area. There, queued up for few minutes as the jabbering crowd shuffles through the lift line, we greet several friends and acquaintances from town and school and work – all joyous as saints, all sporting grins toothy and bright as the Needles Range rising behind us.

Then we're on the lift to the top, my family and I looking, pointing, scheming routes and runs, salivating over the thick, glistening meteorological bounty around us, and staring down enviously on those who hustled up a little earlier than we did as they paint sinuous, sensuous lines down rolling white face of the mountain.

A spectacular blessing of a day. And a rare blessing of a place: a balance of ample space shared by some – but not too many – good people with whom to enjoy it.

And that's why its our favorite little rinky-dink nearby ski area. The way its has been for four decades now.

Of course, the sentiments and situations I have just described, and the way I have described them, are exactly what must drive the movers and shakers and innovators and investors of Durango Mountain Resort, and any wannabe resort (think, say, Red McCombs and his proposed "Village at Wolf Creek") absolutely Freddy Kruger – a money junkie's conditioned response to any sort of long-term economic stasis, restraint, or unfulfilled financial potential.

But these impolite, illogical, and unprofitable sentiments I humbly offer here are out there. Everywhere, in fact, even if there's no seat for these views at the economic-development dinner table, where only food-for-thought digestible by a calculator is served. And there's no better place to catch a whiff of the sweet scent of those anti-growth-and-development perspectives than on the snow-covered limestone stairsteps of Purgatory on a powder day.

You still can catch those because Purgatory is a disappearing breed: a small-time ski area in an era of the big-time year-round mega-resorts. Yet Purgatory, at least for now, remains a throwback: a pretty small, pretty much straight-up skiing-focused 1970s-style ski area – a time when most ski areas were simply small economic pumps that supported remote, affordable mountain communities and the devoted cast of mass-culture outcasts willing to live the life required to really live there. Because of the place itself. And for the companionship – the culture – of others willing to do the same, for the same non-economic, non-quantifiable but highly valuable, highly human reasons.

Today, though, most of the finer mountain towns have been sledgehammered into real-estate brothels, where skiing is just one of the many services rendered to suck a buck from the mountains. enslaved into resorts: juvenilia for the moneyed, urbane urbanite.

Resort development is the West's 21st century extractive industry – social strip mining – disemboweling places to market manufactured "lifestyles" to People of Money, pandering to gluttony, wealth, laziness, and greed while driving the mountain culture out of the towns and into commuting serfdom. It's about generating wealth rather than making a living. And, yes, I do believe there is a big difference. And, no, I don't believe that wealth imbues someone or some group of people with the wisdom, vision, or moral authority to recklessly, ruthlessly, or unilaterally destroy a place and its community for more money.

Blasphemy, I know. But no matter: This being the 21st-century New West and all, there are, of course, grand plans for Purgatory's joining the frenzy, pumping itself up so it, too, can pimp the countryside year round. The first symptoms are apparent from the lift when I crane my neck around: I can't help but note the recent spread of condo cancer and town-home tumors and McMansion malignancy bulging like boils in the woods up and down the valley.
It already feels like the Last Days.

For now, though, Purgatory isn't like one of those Front Range behemoths. In spite of its big-sounding new name, Purgatory is still relatively tastefully adorned with only a simple base area and mountain restaurants, is still surrounded by mostly woods and mountain, and thanks to its location far from an interstate, major airport, metropolitan area – and, often, the jet stream – there are only a few times a year when you have to deal with lines of weekend warriors or wealthy well-suited vacationers.

So even though it drives some insane, Purgatory on a powder day is still mostly just lots of grinning, snow-covered, happy, hillbilly locals. Like us.

At the top of the lift we gather to tighten our boots and coordinate on our first descent. And here a funny thing happens: Webb and Anna appoint themselves guides. Sarah and I can't help but share a knowing glance as we stand there while the kids take it upon themselves to discuss the best plan for staying ahead of the tide of our fellow powder-run seekers.

My wife and I, who have been playing the very same powder-hound games together for two decades now, including the past few years with our kids, sense some kind of rite of passage taking place. Over those years of our sharing so many days with them up here together, we have watched their knowledge and understanding of the mountain grow, their sensing of its moods and snow conditions sharpen, and their observation of the habits of those who use the place deepen. And today, it seems, this training has come to fruition as we listen to our kids negotiate this place. Another wintermark in our "ski trek: the next generation" lives made on Purgatory mountain.

And that's how the day goes, with the kids showing off on the slopes their year of growth in body and mind, and movement further into the world, as Sarah and I follow them down runs, over moguls, and through trees that challenge even our more experienced (albeit another year older) technique. We spend the first couple of hours with the kids leading us down uncut powder-bump lines. With Webb hooting and Anna scooting through powder shots. With their showing us shortcuts through the trees that they'd learned from friends and ski school. With their wending our way back and forth across the many faces of the mountain seeking those lines they know will still be there offering fresh lines even as the day's powder gets eaten by skiers or settled by the sun.

The chairlift rides are fun, too. They are their own sacred shared experience, where we get to sit and talk about school, friends, the day, the last run. Anything. Many things we don't get the time to just sit and chat about in our busy lives at home. Sometimes we just sit, together, quietly. Sometimes the kids ask to ride the lift alone, leaving us to wonder what they're thinking up there, looking around. Other times they ride the chair with strangers with whom they chatter all the way up the mountain.

For most of the day, the kids wait patiently for us at the bottom of each run. This – not their waiting patiently, but their having to wait at all – is another first this year in our shared skiing careers. Another wintermark. And when they get tired of that, we splinter off for our own runs – adults and kids separate – setting up a meeting place and time later.

And Sarah and I feel good about that. Comfortable with that. Happy for them and proud of them and secure with their being able to go off and explore and enjoy this mountain world on their own –

exactly because Purgatory is not another corporate mega-mountain resort-city freak show.

And this year, we feel it: This mountain and its people are now officially theirs. And what more, what better, could middle-aged long-time ski-bum parents want to pass on to their kids? Because to live well, you need places to live well. And to raise good kids, we need good places to raise them in.

But I can't help but wonder what they'll have left to pass on to their kids.

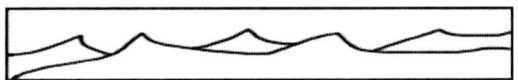

A Pirate Looks at Fortysomething

I didn't plan it that way, but my fortysomethingth birthday was perfect. Perfectly unplanned. Perfectly peculiar. Perfectly apt, representative, symbolic, allegorical, and ceremonial for my life – for my living – as it is in my midlife.

My wife told me early that Saturday morning to do whatever I wanted. A kind and generous gift, but I was staggered for a moment … what does one do given a day to do whatever one will, especially when that day is one's birthday?

I went paddling.

Granted, my birthday is in January. But this is what I did: I grabbed a fat mug of hot coffee, pulled on my old nylon Red Sox jacket, a wool cap and some leather gloves, and I went out to the garage. And there it was: my lonely, dusty red canoe, waiting. I pulled off the things that had accumulated on it since its last venture – sleds, hockey sticks, a broken lamp, boxes of spring-time yard-sale materials – opened the garage door, dragged it out and heaved it up onto the roof of the muddy old truck. I tossed in a life jacket, a paddle, a daypack with some extra warm layers and a few snacks, and drove away.

Happy birthday to me!

I put in on the river on the north end of town and paddled upstream, into the flat, meandering, meadowed reach of river that few people paddle, since most paddlers favor the more challenging swiftwater of town. And there were even fewer boaters than usual on this stretch this January day. No others, actually. Yet the sky was starkly, startlingly clear. The river banks were gleaming snow banks. The meadows were buried under an unbroken layer of winter's freshest. Ravens croaked at me from the bony limbs of skeletal cottonwoods, and the canoe sliced through the cold, viscous water. And not another human soul was out there checking it out with me.

Perfect.

And perfectly me in my forties: Headed upstream.

One of the gifts of being fortysomething is that I can accept this about myself: I'm still the traveler of my youth, but my traveling is different. No longer can I very often lay claim to melodrama, danger, high adventure, or exotic locales. In my forties I've come to accept my world, as both personal reality and historical fact: I live in the 21st century, culturally and terrestially – I have three jobs, two kids, and one house that I can't just pack onto my back and haul to the next valley over yonder whenever I want to explore.

Yet … I travel. Traveling is what I do. Traveling is what I must do. And as a traveler, I crave a regular infusion of irregular places and situations. Every day, even.

So I've adapted my traveling to my circumstances. My traveling today isn't so much heading off the map as it is wandering the little hidden parts of the map. These are those white spaces on your Rand McNally that lie between the main arteries and scenic features – forgotten, ignored, deemed unimportant – like the undramatic and unvisited stretch of the river upstream of town. And like the hundreds of other nooks and crannies of my neighborhood, our town, southwest Colorado, and the Four Corners that I've poked into, wandered around, seen the view from, and slept out in.

While everyone's floating through town, I'm paddling upstream.

At fortysomething, I've also concluded that, for better or worse (or, more accurately, for poorer rather than richer), this traveling mentality also has defined my "career" history. Using our culturally standard resume-style measurement, mine has been a most directionless career path. I've never really settled on any single thing I can say I "do" – which is how we identify ourselves, no? Instead, since the earliest of my working days, I have employed myself with a seemingly erratic array of apparently incongruous jobs, often two or three at once (like now) and frequently changing occupations with the seasons. I can't say it's been easy, and it definitely hasn't been profitable, but it also certainly hasn't been boring.

And that's where I explore at fortysomething: In the white space of our 21st century world, of our 21st century culture, of my 21st century mid-life life. At fortysomething, my traveling is walking away without going away. And the only way is every day.

There is precedent for this. On the dashboard of my van – my road canoe – there stands a three-inch tall Buddha figure. But not just any Buddha figure. This one is not the sitting, passive, somber, dreamy-eyed, ornate and saintly Buddha; this is the dumpy, disheveled, grinning, sandal-footed Buddha with the satchel on a stick hanging over his shoulder – the Traveling Buddha. Legend has it the Traveling Buddha found enlightenment by just walking ... where ever, every where, wandering town to town, meeting people, doing odd jobs, sleeping here and there, checking out the roads, the trails, the woods, the streams, the taverns ... whatever was around.

At fortysomething I've decided I want to be a traveling Buddha. But a 21st century traveling Buddha.

Whatever that is.

m

Later that day, I discovered what that is.

The afternoon of my birthday found me driving out of town with my daughter and one of her friends. This was Anna's request. On my birthday? You bet: What more could I want for at least part of my birthday than to do what my daughter wants?

Especially when what she wants is to go out to Ridges Basin.

Ridges Basin is a broad, bluff-lined, marsh-and-meadow-bottomed valley just outside of town, a nearby refuge for our local wildlife and like-minded humans. It is also another condemned piece of wildland – soon to be submerged under the stilled waters of the Animas-La Plata water project. It's the Bureau of Reclamation's last big Western pork barrel water project, so they're keeping an eye on it: This year, Homeland Security awarded A-LP an extra $2 million just for security because the dam builders think some "terrorists" might go after it.

(Meanwhile my daughter's school this week asked students to bring in pocket change to help buy playground equipment. I ask, what person wanting to hurt our country would be *against* A-LP?)

I hadn't been out there in some time, because the county had closed the access road to allow free reign of the construction companies building the Animas-La Plata Project. I explained this situation to Anna and her friend Abi, but they insisted we give it a go. How could I say no? So after taking the canoe off the truck, we took off toward our doomed destination. It's probably illegal, I was thinking as we headed up a canyon road west of town, but I'm no threat to our country – as in coutryside, as in country living, as in wild country. I'm here to love it.

In only a few minutes, we turned off the pavement and onto a dirt road following the wide, sloping drainage housing Basin Creek. The dirt road soon leads into an area of sage and pinion and juniper and abandoned old ranch buildings. Anna and Abi hooted and cheered when we saw elk – a few dozen loafing in the brown meadow grass, staring indifferently as we rumble by. The loss of Ridges Basin will be an even more painful – even fatal – amputation to them.

After a few miles the snow closed in on the road like a clogged artery. I punched it into four wheel drive, and we slogged on. Then we hit the road closure – and found the gate open. Cheers from the back seat again. There was no one around – although who knows what sort of surveillance toys $2 million can buy – so we rolled slowly on into the middle of the basin. And what I was thinking was, how perfect, again, for my fortysomethingth birthday: Wandering off the map again, to those nearby "upstream" places I love. Even illegally.

The wide, beautiful heart of the basin was a winterland of snow and sage. Low clouds decapitated the surrounding ridgelines, creating a rolling, gray-scale ceiling. We parked in dead middle of this big white space, and got out to wander.

The air was heavy, dense, silent as we – me and these two little apprentice travelers – trudged away from the truck. Once again, we were the sole people to whom it seemed to have occurred to come to this piece of our true homeland.

Anna and Abi knew where they wanted to go. At the top of the hill we found the Bodhi Tree – a Utah juniper, actually, but close enough to the sacred tree for traveling Buddha wannabes like us. And under the Bodhi Tree still sat the old shrine Anna and her friends had accumulated last spring, when we were spending a lot of time out here in our own sort of hospice service for our dying friend, before the damn dam builders locked out the public, before they took this place away.

The shrine is simple: mostly some odd treasures – feathers, rocks, bones, shotgun shells stuffed with wilted flowers – stuff the kids had collected in their travels around the area, honoring the place. The girls carefully cleared away the snow, rearranged the weathered *cositas*, then sat down to write some notes and draw some pictures to the

Bodhi Tree to add to the collection.

Meanwhile, I sat on my haunches and looked past the girls, toward the wide, wild basin – amazingly enough, greater metro Durango sits just over the nearby hills. I studied the new scars the construction work had gouged, work that would soon amputate this place from my daughter and her generation, and their kids. Killing one more nearby faraway.

Then it hit me. Here's my motto, my incantation, in my fortysomething midlife: *To be a human being, be a human doing.* That's the code of the Traveling Buddha. But then I appended that code, to meet the realities of our 21st century world, the world that wants to lock us indoors and off the land: *To be a free human being, be a human doing, no matter what.*

What code is that, then? Well, that, of course, is the code of the pirate. More of a guideline, really ... but still the operational-definition of piracy: treating the world – culture, and place, and your self – as your own, no matter what.

That's the Traveling Buddha today. In the early 21st century, the Traveling Buddha has to be a Pirate Buddha: finding enlightenment by defiantly claiming human terrain in the daily world. And not conceptually, not symbolically – but physically, tangibly, sensually, terrestrially.

The Pirate Buddha walks away without going away every day.

And that's how I found, at fortysomething, that I do have a career after all.

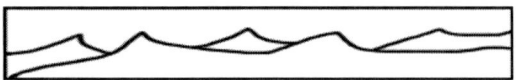

Unmedia Mogul

The revolution will not be televised.
Gil Scott-Heron

*A*ll I can say is, thank the gods these things weren't around when I was a kid.

I mean all those media available to my kids today: iPod, Xbox, CDs, DVDs, cable TV, computers, internet, YouTube, MySpace, Google, emailing, instant messaging, text messaging, cell phones, and whatever other fantastic new miracle of electronic media will hit the market next week.

I'm glad I didn't have those things not because I think they're evil – but because I love those things. As a kid, I would've been an addict.

If I'd had those things when I was a kid, I would've been fully occupied all the time. Which on the face of it would've sounded good back then. I grew up on a rural lake that buzzed in the summer, but which for the three other seasons of the year dwindled in population down to a scattering of mostly widely spaced old folks. So when I grew up, I spent a lot time alone. Having even a fragment of the many media options available today would've meant that I never would've been bored, which I was a good portion of the time as a kid.

But having today's media options when I was a kid would've also meant that I never, or not nearly as much, would've spent my days the way I often did: Exploring aimlessly the shoreline of the lake, in every season, in every mood (both mine and the lake's). Or fishing fruitlessly – but joyously – for hours on end. Or poring through my parents' bookshelves, immersing myself in books I otherwise would never have cracked open (*Pilgrim's Progress*? *Islands in the Stream*? The *Foxfire* series? A five-volume history of World War II? How many kids would plod through those today?). I wouldn't have spent so much time hanging out with my parents and their adult friends. Or sitting at my desk drawing or scribbling for hours. Or wandering through the woods seeing what was out there. Or lying in bed just … thinking. Or tinkering in the basement with hand tools and odd pieces of wood and old broken-down motorcycles and bits of machinery.

And even when there were other kids around, we spent our time playing sandlot baseball or pond hockey or running around the neighborhood making up war games – where, unlike in the organized sports that dominate today, we, ourselves, had to figure out, negotiate, and enforce the rules, and resolve disputes and complaints. And even when we were inside, we were playing board games or collaborating on inventions in the basement or even just sitting around in a real "chat room."

But my kids don't have the problem of having to negotiate their way through boredom, because they have a full smorgasbord of electronic media to fulfill any and every possible craving for distraction and to ward off any potential moment of unscheduled time or unstructured play. It is impossible for them to find themselves in a situation where they would have to ask themselves, What should I do now?

But don't get me wrong – I'm not wallowing in some mire of saccharin "'dem wuz th'days" nostalgia. As a grown-up, I am deeply appreciative of the flexibility, connectivity, and creativity our 21st century mediated world offers us. In fact, these high-tech-tools make possible my cherished mobile, migratory, cobbled-together so-called "career." They keep me informed with things I need and want to know about, keep me in touch quickly and efficiently with those I need to, and with many of those whom I otherwise would let drift off my radar screen. They give me new and novel outlets for my creative endeavors, and access to other artists who would otherwise forever remain obscure to me. And entertainment-wise, I shamelessly enjoy the access to an endless assortment of programming when I want it, as I want it, as long as I want it.

Frankly, I'm glad my kids have this brave new mediated world literally at their fingertips. As a libertarian-leaning pagan-pantheist tribal-anarchist, I honestly believe there's potential and power in these conduits of technological communication being available to so many, so easily, so affordably, and so ubiquitously. In the 21st century world, everybody can be a media mogul.

And I think it's important my kids develop these talents. I want them to be able to navigate and utilize this mediated world deliberately, creatively, adaptably, critically, and with self-awareness. I want them to be able to take on those real media moguls, and corporate rulers, and economic enslavers, and petty tyrants, and government serfs. I want them to be able to use technology to continue the revolution. Or to at least amuse themselves.

But it's a razor's edge: I also want them to know that the mediated world is not the World.

I believe – and here's where I bow and thank those many days of forced boredom I suffered as a youth – that there can be too much entertainment, an excess of information, a glut of diversion, a disconnect stemming from over-distraction. I believe there can just be too much mediation in general – too much filtering through some medium (usually electronic) of our physical, tangible, in-the-moment, where-you-are experiences; and too much pre-processing by some mass media of what those real-world experiences mean.

I believe there can be too little boredom. I believe, if we're not careful, because our media options are now so many, so easy, so affordable, and so, so ubiquitous, that we can too much miss the world that is not filtered and delivered through the media. That is not mediated yet that we are nonetheless really, truly living in. And which is still – for this can never change – the only place where can truly experience truly living.

The unmediated world.

But I'm keenly aware that my kids don't have the historical and domestic circumstances that forced me into that world. And I'm also conscious of the fact that if my kids are anything like me – and I am too often reminded just how much that is so – then they're generally going to choose the mental fast-food of mediated stimulation over boredom's much more nutritious fare. That's what I would've done.

And so I have come to conclude that I – and we, all of us involved in the raising of the next generation that will inherit and inhabit this brave new world of unlimited media and their mixed blessings we have created for them – have an obligation our parents didn't quite so much carry, and probably couldn't have comprehended at all: that the one skill I have the duty to pass onto my kids, and that I believe may well be the most important skill for living in the 21st Century, is *unmediation*.

I want my kids to be aware that the only world that really matters, that is really real, is the one down by the shore of the lake, or out in the woods, or in the yard with friends, or right in the room there with you; that the only world that is really real is not necessarily always the one you can see, but is always the one that brushes your cheek and rustles your hair, that you can wrap your hand around or climb upon or jump into, that touches your lips and you can swirl around in your mouth. It's the world you breathe in. It's the world you live in.

The information revolution is over. Our kids are going to get trained in the media whether we guide them or not – that's a given. They're already better at it than we are. And I'm glad and excited for them.

But I can still teach them how to be skilled at unmediating their world, their experiences. For their sake. Because the next revolution will be remembering how to live, remembering where we live.

And I have a feeling it's not going to be boring at all.

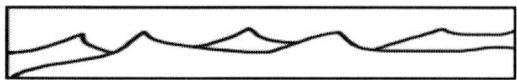

The Discomfort Zone

*M*y son is an addict. And he got it from me, I know. It's scary – he's so young. And now, my daughter's becoming one, too.

I believe this particular addiction is in our genes, if I can use that as an excuse. I know that I, myself, have been addicted as far back as I can remember.

It's never considered healthy to be addicted to anything these days (unless it's to shopping, or celebrity news, or cheap fossil fuels), but I do offer this one justification for this particular bad habit: It's a principled addiction. It's an addiction to a principle. And I believe, if I may discard my usual genteel humbleness for a minute, that it's an addiction that it'd be good for more people to acquire. It might even save the world.

The best part is: I can make a statement of the principle behind this addiction that fits on a bumper sticker – the key to effective and meaningful philosophical discourse today.

But first, let me explain.

Being basically a simple guy, my life, since a very young age, has been guided by a very simple goal: to sleep out a lot. Big deal, you say. Lots of people do that. Some by choice, even. And I agree: it isn't a big deal. As a life-purpose, it offers no financial rewards, social benefits, career advancement, and in no way contributes to my self-esteem or sense of self-worth. Really, it's an occupation and compulsion 10,000 years too late.

But, hey, I didn't plan this. I just, for whatever reason, cannot not sleep out a lot. And somewhere inside I believe that, if I do that, and stick to it, stay true that path, well ... everything else in life will fall into place. It's like, the people and places and situations and conditions that allow me to feed my addiction to sleeping out, well, they are the people, places, situations, and conditions best suited to me anyway.

For this sleeping out, I don't mean living in exotic places, or taking extreme expeditions, or hanging with weird street people, or not working or living in a house or anything. In fact, from my poised, reasonable, prudent outward appearance and rather normal-looking down-town lifestyle, one couldn't even tell that I'm really a zealot, a relentless, unbending stalker of a passion, a pilgrim following an unignorable, uncontrollable vision, a true Calling, however peculiar.

Must ... sleep ... outside.

Beyond that, I try to not complicate life with higher ambitions.

In fact, doing it at home, sleeping right outside my house, or in my neighborhood, or somewhere in some subtle tiny pocket of nearby wildness that everyone else overlooks, well, that's particularly satisfying to my personal obsession. It doesn't matter where I am: If I can get away with it, when everyone else turns in, I will turn out. It's a lazy man's version of poaching the landscape – like those pirate climbers who sneak ascents up buildings and bridges in major cities, or those surfers in the '70s – the Z Boys from California's Dog Town – who took the gentle skateboard and turned it into pavement poaching, riding the concrete land-waves.

Well, my son, Webb, and I are the Zzzzz Boys, treating all the world, even our back yard, like a big campsite. And little Anna is a Zzzz Girl. Since they're kids, they just get it.

I know I got it young. Before school-age, it was pulling the blankets off my bed and constructing tents and teepees with ropes and sticks in the wilderness of my bedroom. Which was fine, but after I went to bed – and my mother always required I slept in my bed, lest I catch the death of something or other – I would crawl down into my little homemade bivouac and sleep there.

In elementary school, I managed, with the help of my father, to convince my mother to let my summer sleepovers with friends be held down in our "breezeway," a screened-in semi-outdoors basement room that overlooked the lake we lived on. My friends loved it – no one else had sleepovers like that.

In middle school, my father added a deck off our house's lakeside face, and so off my bedroom, as well. This was hard to beat, or resist, and I would toss a bedroll out there as many nights as my mother could bear. And many other nights, like back in my bed-side tent-site days, that she didn't know about or approve.

That sneakiness, too, represents the long-term psychological and social impact of my addiction. It's given me a somewhat anarchistic sense of disregard toward the authorities that have tried to legislate and manage my sleeping out – a hobby I've pursued, reverently and with resolve, regardless environment, climate or law, everywhere I've lived and visited.

So what sort of philosophical or political statement am I making by sleeping out with my kids on the little 6-foot by 6-foot deck off our house's second floor? (Which is where I'm headed as soon as I finish explaining this, because there's a boy up there sitting on the deck in his sleeping bag reading Calvin and Hobbes under his head-lamp, waiting for me to join him.)

So what, then, is the point of this discomfort, of the hassle, the weather, the tedious setting-up-and-taking-down of our bedrolls, the sacrificing of nights holding my warm wife in our soft bed?

It's this:

It's a clear night, and warm, just the stars, the air. It's waking up in the earliest gray light, ravens croaking, then falling back asleep. It's water dripping from the blue spruce next to our house after a weak storm – more flash and fury than rain – rumbled through a little while ago. Webb wakes me to see if I want to go in, but I say, no. And he's psyched. We lie there together with drops on our face.

It's a chilly fall night, a sharp moon, some broken backlit clouds. It's bears toppling and rooting through trash cans in the alley all night. It's finding I'm attuned to the changes in the moon and the coming seasons. It's even the vomiting college kid next door, and the drunk stumbling down the street at 3 a.m. yelling undecipherables until someone yells back, "Shut up!"

It's Anna leaving a note on a night that I stay up late writing that says, "Dad, take me outside with you when you go to bed even if I'm asleep!!!" It's Sarah poking her head out to say good night to me and Anna. She laughs when she says, "You guys are crazy!" It's lying there with Webb just next to me, sleeping, his soft breath blending into the gentle night zephyrs.

It's Webb's asking his friend on a sleep over, "Do you want to sleep out tonight?" (And in the interest of fairness and accuracy, his friend's answer was, "Uh … no.")

Hey – it ain't hunting and gathering. And, no, it's not exactly

easy or the most comfortable of addictions. But it also ain't organized sports or video games or Disney Channel. It's not routine, predictable, programmed, scheduled, or virtual. It is always interesting,
invigorating, different, sensuous, and real. Beyond that, though ...
there is no political agenda or philosophical theory or theoretical
stance or preconceived approach. I just really like to be outside.

Hello, my name is Ken, and I am addicted to discomfort.

And so we get, at last, to the principle behind my outlandish
obsession: COMFORT KILLS.

Okay, well, I said it was simple. And, I know, it's not a very dramatic or revolutionary life-guiding principle.

But it does fit on a bumper sticker.

Hunting the
World

Strange as it may seem today to say,
the aim of life is to live,
and to live means to be aware,
joyously, drunkenly, serenely, divinely aware.
Henry Miller

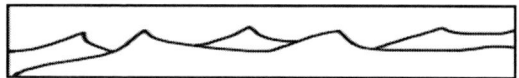

Hunting the World

"You guys have any luck?"

"Hell, yeah!" I chirp out our window and into theirs.

"I mean, neither of us got an elk. Hell, we didn't even see one, did we?" – Matt shrugs his shoulders and smiles at the three guys dressed in blaze orange vests and caps in the other truck – "But we were still successful."

"How so?" the driver asked, looking quizzical.

"No animals … but we moved through some lovely country," I answer philosophically. "And, truth be told, isn't that what we're all really hunting for, after all?"

The three guys look at each other, nodding in agreement.

Then the driver looks back, leaning out his window and beaming with new-found understanding. "Yeah," he says. "I guess you're right."

Yeah. Right.

Truth be told, Matt and I just said, "Nope. No luck," waved, and drove on.

Sometimes, it's just better if people find things by hunting them themselves.

I have long had this peculiar proclivity.

There I am, young and on my own – my friends have taken the road on their bikes – but I walk the three miles of dying New England railroad line from my house to town. Why? Well, the woods, I guess. And the views of the backsides of apple orchards, especially in the fall. And probably the musky and frog-filled swamps that I didn't know if many others saw, but I wanted to see. So I did.

And in college, on the mill-town coast of New Hampshire, there was out the back door of our apartment an abandoned set of tracks. To head south along them strung together the backsides of a half-dozen brick-built towns until the port city was reached. If I headed the other way, turning left out my backdoor, it was five miles to campus – an easy two-hour walk to class. I often made it.

When I moved between those towns along this personal section of rail-line wilderness, I was following a corridor that cut a gently curving swath through oak and maple forest, and bridged dozens of lazy streams and tidal estuaries. Deer still lived there. Ghostly bobcats left lines of prints alongside the rusting rails. Under a particular trestle over a slack river a mile from my apartment, I had stashed a fishing pole and a shovel for worm-digging, and was never denied catfish to bring home for dinner.

After college, following a year of earnest effort at the professional life in Boston – I'm quick to admit my deficiencies, and corporate culture is one of them – I moved West to ski bum for a season. Or twenty five. So far.

I'm still living in the Rocky Mountain West thanks in large part to the fifteen-mile section of the Denver and Rio Grande West Rail Road that is etched into the hard-rock meanders of the Fraser River's Tabernash Canyon. In my first several high-country seasons I got to know the West thoroughly, deeply, and intimately, by moving, and hunting, and fishing, and sleeping out, a lot, along those still-working rails.

Truth be told, I never got an elk there, either – maybe hunting is another personal deficiency – but the fact I'm still out here proves I was successful nonetheless.

I'll skip the literary hunt, and get right to butchering the philosophical prey.

I have a theory: We live in a mediated world.

I don't mean that as analogy or metaphor: I posit that the world we physically inhabit, perceive, act and function within is a manufactured projection that filters for us our experience of the tangible, wild, and self-willing world we were born into and built for.

I further suggest that this mediation is done by the machinery of our Mass Culture, through its physical places, psychic spaces, sensory replacements, and temporal paces. It's how we're raised. It's the way we live. It's our scheduled time. It's what fills our senses. It's what we think about. It's where we're told to go. It's how we get around. Our culture is a machine deliberately designed to hijack our senses, distract our minds, pre-empt our presence, and redirect our attention – to mediate the world.

This process is outlined clearly by the very same diagram I use to illustrate the "communication model" when I teach Introduction to Mass Media: There's a "sender" sending a "message" to a "receiver," but the message must first pass through a "black box," which is the medium – TV, radio, magazine or newspaper, video game, website, etc. And the goal, of course, of any mass medium is to shape the message so as to attract an audience that then can then be delivered to a paying customer.

In the case at hand, the mediating "black box" is everything unique to our present Mass Culture: Our comfortable, convenient, climate-controlled houses. Our quick and efficient transportation. Our non-stop omnipresent smorgasbord of stimuli – the aforementioned TV, radio, music, movies, video games, reading material, etc. It's also where we spend our days: our schools and workplaces, neighborhoods and towns and cities. It's how we are delivered our physical needs: food, and water, clothing and shelter. And it's even our guiding notions of things to be done: Our careers, routines, vacations, educations, retirement plans, self-improvement programs, and even our fully scheduled jam-packed "normal" days.

And what is this "message" Mass Culture mediates for us?

It is, I propose, nothing less than our physical experience of living in the tangible world. And it displaces whatever messages the real Real World is trying to send.

I have kids now. A house to take care of. And a job – several of them, actually. With all that, though, it seems I'm a pretty busy guy. I don't have time to wander the tracks much anymore. But that's okay. I, fortunately have other peculiar proclivities to tide me over.

For example, while I will quickly admit to the deficiency of being a shameless and teary-eyed tree hugger, I like to think I am far from hippie, granola, Rastafarian, or New Ager. Still, I do go barefoot a lot. Around the house. Walking through neighborhoods. Doing errands. Picking up my kids at school. Hiking around the back country. I even climbed a 13,000-foot peak barefoot a couple of summers ago, just to see if I could do it.

I do other stuff, too. I walk to work. (To all my works, in fact.) When I do have to drive, I always drive with the window down, even in the winter when I have to wear gloves and a hat to keep from growing too numb to feel the wheel. Still, I drive as little as possible; to cover that middle ground to places too far or urgent to walk to but not so far as to drive, I recently got a cruiser bicycle. You know: one gear, big seat, fat tires, sweeping handlebars, and a frame that makes you sit straight up. I like it because it's less like riding a bike, and more like driving a slow and hulking car, like a convertible 1967 Cadillac Fleetwood or Olds Delta 88.

Well, maybe more like a 1979 Volkswagen Thing. But it's a cool way to get around anyway.

⌒

I wonder.

Perhaps there was a time when our lives were unmediated: We walked, and hunted, and fished, and every day was fresh and the world itself constantly unfolded in unpredictable, beautiful ways that filled our hunter's senses and surprised our stalking minds.

There's nothing to wonder about now, though: Our lives are not like that today.

But I have a hypothesis: You don't live a life, you live days. And no matter what our Culture attempts to tell you about what matters, our days are the matter that makes our lives.

I want, more than anything, to pass this idea on to my kids. But I'm not sure I have to. You see, my son has been showing peculiar proclivity. He sleeps out a lot. And at least once a week, I join him.

Truth be told, sleeping out is another one of my peculiar proclivities, too. I'm proud to say that while I've, of course, slept out in the backcountry, I've also spent nights in the foothills above Boulder, on a town-home porch outside of New York City, on a picnic table on the plains of Saskatchewan, on a park bench in Germany, in the bushes on a common in a Swiss village, and on the ground in the African Kalahari where I found lion tracks outside my tent the next morning.

But with my son on the little deck outside his room above our backyard has become my favorite place to sleep out. This is because I'm hoping that by doing this with him, by following his lead, that I won't have to tell him my latest theory: That to have the good days that will comprise a good life, you have to have good moments, because moments are the atomic structure of days, and we always – *always* – can choose how we move through our moments.

I'd rather not just tell him that because that would be so much more mediation, would it not? I'm thinking that instead, to be successful, maybe that truth ought not be told. Maybe we'll have our best luck if we just hunt for real moments together.

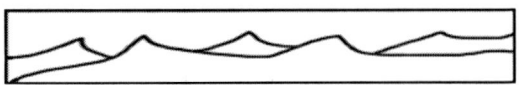

The Most Feral Season of All

*E*aster weekend, the annual Christian celebration of resurrection. An appropriate weekend, then, for our first camping trip of the season. In our family, the year's first Spring nights under the stars mark the rebirth of Summer, which, regardless of how juvenile it may indicate I am, is still one of the most important rituals in my life, right behind our annual Ed Abbey Party, the World Series, the annual San Juan River trip, and winter's first powder day.

Okay, I guess it's not juvenile to love the arrival of Summer. And it's probably no worse than "immature" to have some personal yearly event marking the coming of sweet Summertime. In fact, most human societies for as long as there have been humans to socialize have had communal welcoming festivals for the return of the sun. I guess what's juvenile with me, though, is that I seem to have chosen to take this seasonal switching to a Summer way of seeing things a bit more seriously than most people I know.

I guess what's really immature is that since 1982, the last time I had a single, year-round, full-time job, I have endeavored to build a life guided by Summer – not as a season, but as a perspective, as a philosophy, as a way of living. In fact, I have taken this task a bit farther than our present culture generally rewards with things like money and health benefits and job security. But no use complaining about it (although I still do); it was my choice, and I've come to accept it. At middle age, I've abandoned all delusions of grandeur and am now just hoping that the what Alan Watts once wrote is true: "The bodhisattva is the fool who has become wise by persisting in his folly."

But that's not a discussion for right now, because right now the kids are worth watching: as soon as we pull into our campsite, even before the engine is off, they leap from the car and run loops around the cottonwoods, joined by our cooped-up dog, who is doing laps around both the kids and the cottonwoods. By the time my wife and I climb out of the car and walk over to greet our other friends, who had arrived earlier in the afternoon, the kids and the dog have already sprinted up the sandy wash, scaled and leapt off the steep dirt rim above camp, and gathered in a pack with their friends (canine and human) and loped up onto the gentle slickrock slopes at the foot of the high sandstone escarpment in the distance.

Regardless of how much I myself need this trip, watching the kids reminds me of why we're really here: to get feral. Once you've got a dose of Summer, at any time of year, you just add a tent and a campfire, then mix it in the backcountry somewhere for a few days, and you've got the recipe for feralness.

Kids need no guidance in this transformation; the most helpful thing a parent can do is not interfere (except in safety matters), and let them just see and do as they will. Even when our kids were little our general camping-trip policy was to bring only buckets and shovels for toys. Our experience has been that letting the kids just play with the landscape leads to far less boredom, far fewer arguments, and far more surprises, discoveries, and adventures for all involved.

In fact, I believe (based on no empirical experimentation, but on strictly personal observation and gut feeling) that it takes years of relentless practice, formal training, and persistent education to turn a wild little human critter into a civilized grown-up citizen who can rationalize away Summer's callings and instead say, "Yes, I'd rather be inside a lot during the summer, especially on a most grand and glorious day, so I can own many things and get 150 channels on TV and drive a new car that goes faster than I'll ever need to drive and pay lots and lots of money for frantically-paced vacations for two quick weeks, if I'm lucky, in places I'd love to live in."

Some of us, though, it seems, arose from a strain of the human species resistant to this enculturation. But that's a story for another time, because while I've been carrying on, dinner has been prepared and eaten, dusk has given way to twilight, and nighttime is on deck. The seven kids on this trip join the grownups around the campfire. It's time to award the kids this year's rite of passage: They are ready for their own little campfire.

They are ecstatic at the news. The kids help collect a woodpile and build a smaller version of the grownups' fire ring, and they stand around big-eyed as I light a real honest-to-goodness fire in it. We put a couple of the more mature kids (read: girls rather than boys) in charge, and the little tribe pulls their little chairs into a little social circle. Then we adults leave them to themselves; we withdraw to our own fire circle, where we can conveniently and subtly watch the rookie fire.

For the next couple hours we share chuckles at glimpses of the kids sitting around chatting, laughing, poking the coals, tossing on more twigs and sticks, visibly exulting in the responsibility and significance and the honor of this event. The sight reminds me that in a few years, a few more rites of passage down the trail, these kids will be out here on their own, by boat and boot and beater car with a half-a-million miles on it and loaded with water and beef jerky and warm canned beer. They'll be seeking their own paths to feralness. As long as they still have places to get out, that is – yet another (not that we need another) non-economic argument for preserving wilderness and wild country: it's our spiritual bank, our feral reserve system....

But I'll gripe about that some other time, because for now my parental musings are broken by our white lab, who struts into the fire circle, spins a few tight turns, then curls up at my feet into pile of crusty fur that reeks like week-old road kill. Speaking of feralness, I think, as I nudge her away from the fire and into the olfactory isolation of the bushes some yards away.

She gives me a confused and offended look, then resigns herself to the cold loneliness of her campfire exile. Can't blame her. It's not her fault, of course. Although she's a "goofy," a creature selectively bred right out of her gene pool, somewhere there is some latent programming humming away that makes her still find great canine joy, purpose, and satisfaction in covering herself with a rich coat of maggoty, decaying flesh or the ripe green ooze of a fresh cowpie.

And who am I to criticize that? I mean, in a sense isn't that what the kids are doing? Isn't that what I've spent my life doing? The lingering lure of feralness calls to even the most domesticated of us. But we can still choose to go feral – to be our own anti-domestication movement. Isn't that why I've never been able – and I tried once – to work full-time in the Summer at anything other than commercial river guiding, regardless of the economic insanity that choice introduces into my civilized life?

It's because Summer is just too brief and precious to spend indoors. It's because summer reminds me just how ephemeral life in general is, so I should never piss away a day. In fact, after some 20 years of pursuing this Summer perspective, I can safely say the goal of my life, my highest ambition and aspiration, my career as much as I have one, is to grow increasingly feral – working hard at unlearning how I was taught to live in the world, and relearning how to follow the compass of my conscience.

Kids, perhaps because they haven't been trained against it for as long, don't have as far to go as adults do to align themselves to these instinctual compass bearings. "I wish we could live here," Anna says to me the next morning. Then she and one of the younger girls go back to work: They're diligently lettering signs with markers on pieces of scrap lumber that were brought for firewood. After a day and a half at this, scattered around our camp stand a series of these cryptic little wooden tablets scribbled with kiddie catchphrases, like "I love you and you love me to," and "Evry budy has fun with ech othr."

And then there's another young one, this one a boy, sitting alone in the wash like he's starring in a desert version of *My Side of the Mountain* (My side of the Arroyo?). He doesn't see me as I watch him inspect a series of pebbles in his hands, then runs his hand through the wildflowers hanging over the side of the wash, all the while mumbling to himself like a mantra over and over: "Oh, I like this place so much…."

Webb, on the other hand, perhaps because he's my child, seems to be swimming in the deep end of our gene pool. I'm in awe of his focus and effort – not always his strengths at school – as he and the other boys work for hours at chipping sandstone rocks into spear points, which they then affix to sticks with rubber bands and bits of string they gathered from under car seats and in kitchen boxes. They then spend the rest of the afternoon hunting lizards, unsuccessfully but relentlessly, occasionally discussing strategy and regularly cheering each on in pursuit of the elusive prey….

Growing increasingly feral. It doesn't take much.

Time to do my part: I take off my shoes and spend the rest of the weekend barefoot. Another juvenile Summer habit I never managed to outgrow: more than by the size of my bank account, I measure the quality of my life by the quality of my feet. Are they tough? Are they tanned? Are they alive and sensitive and in contact with the earth? If I can answer "yes" to those questions, then I know I'm doing something right. Because in the feral view of things, the sole is a window on the soul.

Time to get on that project, then, because it's already Summer, even in the spring. Soon my teaching job will be over, and I'll spend the next four months or thereabouts scraping for odd jobs – writing, running rivers, teaching workshops, maybe pounding some nails. More importantly, though, those jobs will be woven around my and my family's getting out, a lot (my wife works in the schools, too) – the annual San Juan River trip, a couple of weeks traveling there, a few days backpacking or car camping here, whenever we can.

It'll be Summer, after all.

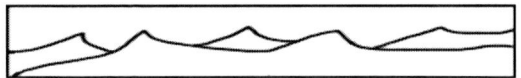

Letter From a Paleo-Dad

W ebb;
I can't imagine what you're going through these days. A teenager. Good gods! What a great, crazy time … What a vital, crazy time.

I, of course, have, as they say, been there. But you're going through this in a world as different as an alien planet on Star Trek from the world I was in as a teenager. But that is the nature of the times.

So I can't imagine what it's like for you. But I explore there when I can.

That's why I took the day off to join your class on its field trip the other day. All the years I've been here, I had never been to the Anasazi Heritage Center, so it was cool to see it. I have to admit, though: as cool as it was, it kind of shook me up. I'd already been thinking a lot (I think too much, your mother says) – thinking about you, about what you're going through, about what you're going to be going through in the next several years. About what *we're* going to go through.

And with that, I'd been wondering how I can be a good father, to you and your sister, now and in the years before you begin your own lives, on your own. So, my mind was already churning that day. But something about that day, with you and your class at that museum, hearing stories about those ancient people and how they lived a millennium ago here, in the Four Corners, right where we live, really sent my mind off.

But I think I hid it well. Did you notice? While we were walking I shuffled along politely with everyone else. And when we – you and me and a few dozen of your classmates, a bunch of teachers, and a few of us parent chaperones – stopped to hear a teacher discuss how the Anasazi used a plant or a mineral, or something about how they hunted or prepared food, or about what a ruin said about ancient daily life, well, I tried to be a good role model of patience and attention.

What I really wanted to do, though, was to bolt off on a dead run through the pinion-juniper (great source of food!), leaping yucca (used for making sandals!), and disappear over the hill (site of a small pueblo!) yelling wheeeehaaaa! I really wanted to eat those pinion nuts. I craved to strip that yucca to weave some of those sandals. I hungered to catch a rabbit with an oak-branch trap and roast it for lunch, then nap off the meal in the restored pit house. After that, I wanted to grab the kids and the grownups and hang out together chipping flint arrowheads or grinding cornmeal while we laughed and told stories. Later, I thought maybe we'd have a great ceremony around a big fire, telling scary tales about the great ghosts – those "talking heads" that come out of boxes in our houses – that endeavor to corral us indoors and apart from the rest of our tribe.

But I think too much.

Still, I know you get it. When I whispered my idea to you, you laughed out loud. But we both know that the days of living like that are over – a lot has changed since the ancient ones lived here. That's why this stuff is in a museum. Now what do we do? Well, we go to a museum and talk about the stuff in the glass cases. Or we stare at the interactive software that shows what people did back then, outdoors, on the land, with their hands, with each other, every day. Or we walk around the museum grounds while someone points to a plant – don't touch! Stay on the paved walkway! – and tells us what people who lived on the land did with that plant. And we take notes because there's a quiz tomorrow.

And then what? Then we go back to the school. I leave you with your teachers so you all can go back indoors and sit quietly and talk about what you saw and talked about. For a break, you'll get your 20 minutes to eat your lunch from a box, then you can run around outside for a half an hour until the bell commands you head back inside to sit and talk and study some more.

Hey, don't get me wrong: I think your teachers are tremendous, given what they have to work with. And I know you have some fun at school – you, like I did, will have good, important, shared experiences going through school with your friends. And I think the school you attend is about as good as it gets. But: School is the way it is these days; and the way it is, no matter how much your teachers work to make school "hands-on," the fact is school amounts to sitting indoors quietly and orderly (or else!) all day every day, talking about and seeing images of and reading about the world "out there." School is, in a nutshell, a great, big, all-day, 12-year-long visit to a museum.

But I think too much.

But I know you get it – you've told me so. You've told me you'd rather be doing things every day – exploring, stalking, learning by doing, facing trials, making errors, wandering, loafing, honing skills, outside, out there … No curriculum, no program, no list of academic objectives to check off. You'd rather just go … just do …see what you find … learn by coming back with questions.

But that, of course, ain't the nature of school. And, take my word for it, from someone who's been out in the world after school for a quarter of a century, the things they really teach in school – self-control, focus, rule-following, routine, boredom, inactivity, "studying" instead of really experiencing – that's the training you'll need to survive the "normal" world we live in today. We don't live anymore like those hunters and gatherers – the way people lived for 99 percent of human history.

Still, again, don't get me wrong. Even if that's what I think, here's what I know: Just because the way we live has changed, we are still humans. And here's what else I know: we still live in a wonderful, exciting, mysterious, glorious, fantastic, kick-ass world, filled with a crazy, strange, beautiful variety of people.

That's why I'm writing you this letter. I've thought a lot since I joined you on that field trip to the Anasazi Heritage Center. And here's what I came up with:

Your teachers are good at what they do – teaching you how to make a living today. That's their job. But: My job is to teach you how to live.

So, given that, I then thought, as a father what can I learn *from* the Anasazi, rather than *about* the Anasazi? I wondered: What would an ancient father say to his teenaged son? What could we both say about how to live a good life that would be meaningful in either time? What could I say that will be useful tomorrow – in the world you'll live in that I can't possibly predict?

Well, here's what I came up with. Four guidelines, four compass bearings, four sensibilities rather than rules, four things fathers would want to impart to their kids anytime, anywhere. Four things I seek to teach you:

- **Do things.** You don't have to do everything, but do lots. Sample doing some things; some things, follow through to absurd, deep, powerful ends. Learn how to do things for yourself. Admire and learn from people who do things you can't. Do the things you ache to do. Do things that make you feel good. Do things that don't make you feel good, too, but that you know are good things to do anyway. Sometimes, do nothing. Regardless, no matter what you do, do things for the doing, and do them your way.

- **Get out.** That means outside, of course. Get out of doors, often, regularly, daily. Sleep out. Walk. Explore your neighborhood. Open the window. Take the long way home. Travel far and wide. Also travel near and deep. Beyond that, though, "get out" also means get "out" of whatever keeps you "in" – routines, habits, fears, comfort, the ideas of others, ideas of yourself. Know that every moment is a chance to be more than others – and even you yourself – think you are, and "out there" will always be right here.

- **Honor tribe.** First, seek your tribe: those with whom you have a connection beyond the circumstances that brought you together. Those who see the world you see. Those who need the world you both see. And when you find those people, get to know them, and let them know who you are. Explore each other – see who they are, regardless of who you wish they were. And then, stand by those relationships. Remember: your relationships don't belong to just you – they are not yours to manipulate for your needs. Know this: How you treat your relationships defines who you are. And what you are. That is honor. Do that – always honor others – and those relationships will be there when you need them. And then you'll always have a tribe.

- **Abandon yourself.** To everything. All the time. No matter what. Abandon to what's in front of you right now. Always. Abandon yourself to your Self – to your style, to what you must do, to who you cannot not be. Abandon yourself to those you love – and give them the space to abandon to themselves. Have faith. Be sincere. Yes, you will be hurt. You will make painful mistakes. Abandon anyway. Sometimes the hardest way will be the best way; other times you'll get such great good fortune that you'll feel balanced on the biggest wave – abandon to that, too, and ride it as long as you can. And remember: no matter what circumstances you find yourself in, no matter what happens to you, no matter what others do to you, you are always in control of your attitude. You, and you alone, are responsible for your journey. Abandon to that most of all.

That's it, really. Those are what I want to teach you. Vague, but specific enough to apply any moment. Simple, yet you can spend your whole life honing those skills. These directions fit today, yet they could guide a thousand years ago. And they guide me now, as I face the next few years as your father.

And so I abandon to this: I don't know if I can be a good father, but I can father good. I can best "father good" by honoring you, by helping you be who you are. I can best help you find who you are, not by showing or telling you what to do, but by just doing things with you, just getting out with you.

And, like fathers, teachers, and sages have said to their kids, students, and apprentices for eons, I will stay and do that with you – not until the end, because that journey is yours – but until the beginning.

Until you abandon to your own journey.

Until then, my job is to take off running through the world with you.

I know you'll get it.

Dad.

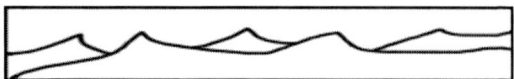

Done With Magic

Listen. Below us. Above us. Inside us.
Come. This is all there is.
Terry Tempest Williams

*T*ime to grow up. Now that I have lived long enough, observed widely enough, and seen enough of the results of the many quaint, bewitching notions that soothed and comforted me for most of my life, it is time to shed those myths and superstitions.

I don't believe in that magic anymore. I'm done with fantasy. With dreaming. With following mirages born of hopes and schemes. I've learned, instead, that there is a real world that functions regardless of the ideas I might impose in its place; that there are ways of doing things that work, and ways that, no matter how many wishes are cast in their path, do not; that consequences follow our actions like a wake, no matter how much we rationalize away the ripples.

And I've learned that I have too long been placing my faith in mystical powers and forces that I believed guided us and dictated how we best should live. But don't.

No more. Now I believe only in things I, myself, test personally and verify experientially, and I'm done with anything that doesn't pass that muster.

I don't believe, for example, that "success" is the goal; I no longer believe in wealth, worth, titles, or awards. Instead I believe in style, skill, resolve, and honor, because they're tangible, doable, and cannot be faked.

I don't believe in making a living; I believe in making a life.

I also now believe, again from experience, that getting old, despite it's physical challenges, is really pretty cool. Even despite its inevitable ending. Because I believe in what the Universe so clearly says everywhere: Everything changes; nothing ends.

I now believe that, despite the government's repeated denials and claims of ignorance, that, yes, aliens really do live among us. For only a few months of the year, though, and for the rest of the time their space-station-sized second homes often stand empty, waiting, idling, while they're away, in outer space.

I believe that most real heroes are not celebrities.

Speaking of celebrities, I don't believe Barry Bonds. But that's just a hunch.

I also have a hunch that naming that car a "Hummer" was not just a Freudian slip.

I, of course, it almost goes without saying, don't believe that economic growth is good. I don't even believe that "growth is inevitable," no matter how much that incantation is chanted in the newspapers and county commissioners meetings and city council chambers.

I believe we can live differently.

And I believe we have to, because I believe Malthus had it right.

Unlike Machiavelli, whom I don't believe had it right.

I do believe Jesus had it right, however. And I don't believe that He was somehow mistaken or misquoted when he pointed out that "it is easier for a camel to go through the eye of a needle, than for a rich man to enter the kingdom of God."

I also believe that I, myself, will not get the chance to test that theory.

I do believe that although might might make wealth, it still doesn't make right.

And I still believe that while the so-called "global economy" may claim to have magically made the world "flat," sending jobs overseas isn't right, either.

I believe that plants, animals and rivers have rights equal with our own.

I also believe in the rights of unborn children – in fact, I believe we should respect those rights for seven generations ahead. Which pretty much casts a pall on plastics, nuclear power, land development, and the aforementioned growth-based economy.

Speaking of children, I don't believe our already-born children – those young, eager, curious, seeking, learning little mammals in their most formative years – should be locked in big, bland boxes we call "schools" all day.

I don't believe skateboarding is a crime. But I believe Glen Canyon Dam is.

Yet I believe that in my lifetime I will see Glen Canyon restored to its wild and wonderful three-dimensional, redrock glory. I also believe this might take a miracle, but I didn't say I was against *all* magic.

I no longer believe recycling is going to save the world. Or that listening to NPR or joining an environmental group makes one an activist. I believe only action does.

And I don't believe you can ever say "I'm just doing my job."

I no longer believe we can magically fix the problems caused by what we've done by just doing it more, and doing more of it. I believe we have to live differently.

And I believe we can.

I believe we can not because I believe in schemes, schedules, plans, programs, or pogroms. I don't. I also don't believe in a sealed fate. I do, however, believe in abandon. And in adaptation. And in the ongoing revolution of evolution – because everything changes but nothing ends, forever and ever, amen.

And I believe in our human ability to create culture, from scratch if need be. And I do not believe that culture is created on TV, or in Congress, or on Wall Street. I believe culture is created in individual choices.

I believe I have found the Weapons of Mass Reconstruction, and I believe they are in each and every individual choice, voice, and action done with style, skill, resolve, and honor.

And I believe that even though that doesn't take magic, it is still the most magical thing of all.

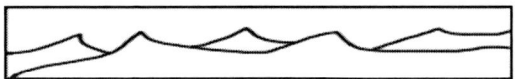

The Little Things

*I*t's the little things, I'm thinking as Webb and I walk up along a little creek.

We came up here on a whim. Sarah and Anna are off on some foray together, so this evening Webb and I threw some food and warm clothes into the van and started driving. "I want to sleep where I can hear a waterfall," Webb stated as we drove away, offering the only parameters we had to work with.

We didn't have to drive far. Just a little ways out of town we found a little dirt county road that lead to an even littler, even dirtier Forest Service road that lead up a little little-known drainage. Soon we were parked, and the sliding door of our Chevy kiva was opened to the big sound of the little creek rolling over rocks.

Across the valley from our parking spot a trail winds up along a rushing side creek, and we follow it. It's early summer, so Larkspur blossoms bloom violently violet against the green undergrowth, and the aspen and cottonwoods are leafed out, lime green and savoring their first big sips of sunlight. A bar of early evening light beams down the notch of the narrow valley, illuminating rock outcroppings and reaches of the noisy, fat stream.

While we're walking through this simple beauty, Webb is, as they say, off in another world. He wanders off the trail, picking his own most-indirect routes, mumbling to himself and sword fighting with a stick and … manifesting whatever else is going on in that young brain of his. It's like watching a dog dream – who really knows what fantasy adventures we're witnessing the shadows of? For Webb this whole landscape is a natural obstacle course and toy box. While I'm dutifully walking on the designated trail and fully "in my senses," I sense that, even if Webb's play isn't practical, intellectual, or rational,

THE MONKEY WRENCH DAD

it is nonetheless his way of seeing the world. He's still interacting with the creek, crawling over rocks, touching the pieces of burnt wood left over from recent fires. Through playing, he's not in "another world" – his play is his portal to *this* world as a world. And I interact in my own way, on a slow, aimless stroll, just smelling and looking and feeling the air on my skin. That's my play.

The sun has fallen below the ridgeline above us. Cool air slides down the valley and washes over us. We need to turn around even though the trail makes us want to keep going – that familiar ache of paths not followed.

We return to our camp and share a fire under the stars, sipping sodas, and chatting, and often not-chatting, just enjoying the silent space. Finally we crawl into our sleeping bags in the van. Before we fall asleep, Webb looks up at me with his dirty face (and therefore, by operational definition, a happy face), and states, "Dad, we like the same kinds of fun, huh?"

And right then I know that if I had only one night in the world to pass with Webb, I would pass on the Disneylands and the Eiffel Towers or even the Grand Canyons, and this is the blessing I would choose.

It's the little things.

ur

If there has been any thread through my life, it is this: a life of love of little places.

My memory is littered with them. As a kid, it was the trail (called just "The Trail") through the woods (called , of course, "The Woods"). For my adolescent consciousness, it was home to adventures, stories, games, explorations, dangers, risks, meditations, visions, and dreams. This little place was enormous on that plane. It was inseparable from who I was. It's also where I pulled up my first survey stakes – a completely instinctual, thoroughly non-ideological act of self-defense – so I guess it was also inseparable from who I was to become.

Since moving out and on my own, where ever I found myself living I also found myself stalking the little nooks and crannies that few others seek or see. In the worst of times, no matter how crazy my life has gotten, no matter how broken my heart or dashed my plans or vague the trail, I have always found sanctuary in little places where I could re-create myself in the lonely but not-alone comfort of just me and the out there. And in the best of times, finding those spaces reminds me that the blessings in this world aren't just given, they're chosen.

I have chosen the five miles of railroad tracks I walked alone from my apartment to my classes at the University of New Hampshire ... the high-country canyon near Winter Park I hiked while my ski-bum friends skied ... nights camped in my van up in Ridges Basin outside of downtown Durango honoring the latest little wild place martyred to yet another wasteful Western water project. And on and on.

Because I believe that it's in these little places where the real intimacy – with the land, and with ourselves – takes place.

It's the little things, I'm thinking, as Webb is feeding peanuts to camp robbers – they're flitting right up to him and eating from his hand. His face flickers between joy and awe.

It's the end of summer now, and where we are is on a two-day backpack trip, this time with Sarah and Anna along, in the high country north of town. The approaching winter had shot out its first tentacle yesterday, as a quick, dense, chilling storm that left a few inches of high-country snow in its wake. So, on another whim, we decided to check it out – another cheap nearby adventure. So here we are, four of us in a line tromping along under our backpacks through slushy snow.

We're at the tundra-covered base of a grand, blanched peak, like a great molar. Around us stands an enormous horseshoe of luminous, numinous mountains. What I'm admiring out there are called "postglacial features" – cirques, U valleys, moraines, tarn lakes, etc. – by the scientific community. Being an incorrigible optimist, though, I see pre-glacial features.

On closer range, though, the optimist in me is challenged. It's just little things – like the often deteriorating and sometimes missing trail signs that indicate a general neglect by the federal land-management agencies entrusted these lands. But to me they mark the trail toward bigger things: the movement toward fee-generating campgrounds and RV-pandering pavement and gadget-buying ORVers and profit-turning concessionaires and "corporate partnerships" that are increasingly the "public" in public lands these days. On our public lands today, it seems our government is issuing corporate America a license to shill – up for grabs next are the remaining roadless areas, timber, oil, gas, coal, resort development, and the fees that can be extorted from hikers and campers. And, as the logical terminus of "it's just good economic sense," the selling off of public lands.

When it comes to money, it's the big things.

But we must not forget: aside from their economic value, it's the little places – and tons of them – that our public lands preserve. It's not the income they can generate, nor the tourists they can attract, or the recreational opportunities they might offer that justify the keeping of our public lands free and accessible and undeveloped. It's just the commons. That alone is enough. That is the point of our public lands: They are refuges of the little places that offer the little things that most of us need but not all of us can afford. And that none of us should have to afford.

But, I remind myself, I am an optimist. So I turn my attention back to my kids. As we crest the divide at the base of the peak and move on toward the drainage on the mountain's backside, Anna is leading our pack. From behind, she is just two little legs descending from a red canvass bag, but her stride is that of some pack animal. Webb, meanwhile, appears, as usual, "in another world."

Still, when I point to a nearby peak and say "Jura Knob," he responds, "No, you're a knob, dad." He is the happy wanderer, singing and brushing his finger against the stunted trees. In his Thoreauvian "different drummer" sort of way, his happy gait exhibits the strong-and-relaxed, comfortable-yet-aware mood that indicates a different kind of self-confidence than one gets from, say, being good at video games, or from dressing cool, or from school test scores.

And if I want to pass anything on to my kids, it is that. That, and the places that offer that.

Of course, that may take some work, some risk, some effort at getting involved. But I also know that it is in the present we choose the blessings that the future will be given. And we can choose the blessing of public lands for our children's future, because we – every one of us – owns our public lands. Still. For now.

And every one of us can pass on that inheritance, if we are willing to do whatever we can wherever we are to defend our public lands and care for the little places we love. If each and everyone of us does something, no matter how small.

Because it's the little things.

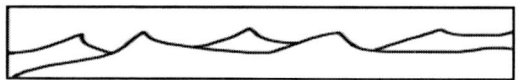

Following in Their Parents' Fall Lines

My wife and I have a Sunday ritual: We roust ourselves and the kids from bed early (that's not the most appealing part), grab some coffee and bagels, throw our ski stuff in the car – our tele skis in the roof rack and the kids' alpine gear in the back – and cruise the 20-minute shot up the glorious Animas Valley to Durango Mount– ... uh, Purgatory. How 'bout that national-park quality commute, eh? The ridiculous Hermosa Cliffs, like stone aurora. The ragged tear of the Twilights in the flat morning sunshine. The well-walked slopes and bands of Engineer Peak – the ascending of which is a summer ritual. For me this drive is a religious experience every time, and church on Sunday.

We blaze up to the mountain so early for Snowburners, Purgatory's weekly ski school for local kids. And local it is: Standing around in the snow at the base of the ski area each week, Sarah and I can catch up with a month's worth of acquaintances and friends just in the time it takes the kids to find their groups – where they also run into to their own friends from school and all over town. Like in an old village square on market day, we hang around chatting, generally in no hurry to head off on our own day of skiing as we suck up the cold, crystalline mountain morning.

These Sunday mornings are a tincture of mountain-town culture (or at least the skiing subculture, just one of the many intriguing tribes found in a mountain town). It's a culture that, in the vein our species' tribal roots, has coalesced around a place that matters to them, and lives a lifestyle that maximizes getting out in that place as much as possible. The places offering this lifestyle, though, are by nature and definition not always easy places to make a living, so these Sunday morning ski-area gatherings are healthy reminders of what making as much money as possible was sacrificed for. They are medicine.

I've experienced other such mountain-town ceremonies – the many ski area jobs, the months of hostel-living, the out-of-bounds adventures (not that I endorse such illegalities), the Thursday 25-cent draw nights at the Crooked Creek Saloon in Fraser, Colo. (the only place, to my memory, where I've ever danced on a table with a professional belly dancer), and the thanks offered to Üllr, the Norse god of snow, for any powder day regardless of whether one can get out and play in it or not.

Still, there is something particularly meaningful about the Snowburners ceremony, something particularly significant for the present (read: parental) state of my ski-bumming career: Snowburners is about the kids.

On each Sunday from January though March, these kids go to the mountains to join this congregation at ski school: their ski-culture apprenticeship. Born of former ski bums, this next generation of snow riders is studying under the present generation of ski bums. And when these kids get together each week to shred, they're also learning the spirit that spawns this culture – the magic of that controlled abandon to the fall line, and the power that comes from trusting yourself to ride that abandon. It's a philosophy, an attitude toward life – and it's also what binds this group of people as much as mountain and snow. And every Sunday when that mountain-town spirit is passed on, I can see the tribe evolve right before my goggles.

A few weeks ago Webb and couple of his friends were riding up to Snowburners together, when the others started griping about the early morning, the cold air, how they didn't want to ski today, etc. Can't really blame them – weekend mornings are precious, lads.

"You guys!" Webb finally interrupted. " It's a powder day!"

Yes! Surrender to the fall line of the day, son! It's enough to make a ski-bum parent teary.

And it's not just skiing. That fact that passing on the culture was what was happening, here and in other things we do with our kids, was revealed to me last summer on the Green River, in northwestern Colorado. Earlier in the summer, we had been asked to join in on this five-day float, even though we knew only one of those going, and even him not very well. We wondered why, but grabbed at the chance.

Our first night on the river, we found out why we were there. We were camped in a box elder grove in a deep, sheer part of Ladore Canyon. That night, after the kids had gone to bed (our kids were the only ones on the trip), we sat around a fire on the beach as the river slid by, black and silent as oil. The night was so dark it hurt to look at the stars.

"You just gotta have kids on a river trip," Bill explained to us, grinning into his rum punch. And that was it. That was enough. All present agreed with his view.

"All" means Bill and his bunch of long-time river-rat accomplices. These six folks – Sarah and I were the third and fourth youngest after our two kids – first began running rivers together back in the '70s, when they all lived in Silverton. And they had stories to tell of those days. Of skiing the same backcountry runs we still ski, and of running the Four Corners rivers we run with our kids today. Other stories, though were the tales of a different time, another world: anecdotes and reminisces of floating that very Green River before Flaming Gorge Dam, of running the Dolores River before McPhee Dam, of sailing the surging San Juan before Navajo Dam, of savoring the Gunnison on its last free-flowing day before the penstocks were closed on Blue Mesa Dam. And other memories: of a tiny, tough Telluride ... of our beloved Winter Park before it aspired to "world class resort" status ... of Purgatory when it was small and local.

Okay, Purgatory is still small and local – there's nothing like a week-day powder day when you know most of the people riding Lift 8, each recognizable under their weather-armor just by their distinctive gluttonous grins. That, in fact, is part of why Sarah and I live in southwestern Colorado rather than somewhere near one of the mega-resorts outside of Denver or Salt Lake City. Still, reflecting on those elders' stories since that Green River trip has made me cringe even more whenever those too-familiar alarms ring in the newspaper: The Animas-La Plata Project gets more millions in tax dollars from Congress ... the Dolores Water Conservation District wants two more dams for the Dolores ... some billionaire wants to build yet another mega-resort on the remote and wilderness-abutting Wolf Creek Pass ... Purgatory's new owners have changed its name to "Durango Mountain Resort" with aspirations for yet another "year-round world-class resort."

It's enough to make a still-skiing, still-a-river-rat, still-mountain-town-living-ski-bum parent weep.

My point here isn't to whine, though. Really. Why bother? That this is happening is not news. We all know what we're up against. And even though I hope we're all doing what we can to resist, I also think we all know our chances. Whining is of no use, but the fact is you can't help thinking about the future without getting to the part about how our towns are getting too expensive to support a bum culture, about how the little ski areas are all turning into expensive and low-paying "world-class resorts," about how our public lands and rivers and open spaces are still being devoured by the cult of economic growth and development. We know ... but no one likes to talk about it all the time – it's like that elementary school joke, "Shhh ... it's around the corner."

I'm also one of those who doesn't want to hear it all the time. Besides, as a parent, I'm generally an optimist – I've made my genetic wager on the side of the future. So what to do? Well, here's what I'm going to do: Sure, I'll keep up my quixotic fight to keep our towns affordable, our public lands public, our rivers free flowing and free – that fight in me seems to be a genetically programmed reflex: propose it and I oppose it. What I'll also be working on meanwhile, though, is passing on what cannot be buried under resorts, flooded by dams, or marketed to a wealthy clientele: The culture. The Tribe. More importantly: The spirit that seeds those weeds anew in whatever soil is available.

Teach the kids to abandon to the fall line – savor whatever life offers here and now, the people, the places, the circumstances – and they'll handle whatever terrain they encounter in their own runs through the world that awaits them.

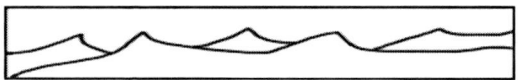

Old and Going Downhill Fast

*T*his story goes to show that you *can* teach an old dog new tricks. It's just a good idea if he wears padding and a helmet when you do.

Which I do, being an old dog, as I ride my longboard across greater metropolitan Durango on a cool early-autumn night under the dull monsoon-masked luminescence of the full moon. Or fool moon, maybe, for I am accompanied by a pack of my fellow middle-aged fools, passing three wee hours on a backcountry-style foray into the ultimate front country, the open slopes and trafficked glissades of our home town's urban neighborhoods.

We're kicking and gliding and riding our way from the east side of town, across the rich-scented rain-swollen Animas River – the soul of Durango – and then up, up, and farther up the rumpled network of streets that spill out from the foothills of Perins Peak. Tonight that sandstone monolith stands as a dim swelling above the highest threads of pavement rising from the glittering glow of town.

When we gain this uppermost reach of Durango's road system, a dark cul-de-sac in a narrow ravine, we stop, turn, and stand, to catch our breath and take in the scene. The lonely road leads into near-nothingness, since the moon has slipped deeper under the cover of the growing cloudmass. And it has begun to rain, lightly, but enough to already give the street sloping away at our feet a sheen of reflected city-glow from Durango proper, a galactic mass of light below us.

And we confront our task: to cruise and carve a series of long runs down through this tamed landscape, back to the river.

A new trick for me, this skateboarding. For most of the guys I'm with here, though, aside from my friend Jan, who has agreed to join me on this adventure in juvenilia, longboarding is an old trick. For the past few months, he and I have embedded ourselves in this band of boarders to get a crash (or, mercifully, so far, no-crash) course in pavement poaching. Tonight is our graduation party of sorts.

Even I'm surprised to be here. All my life, I'd never felt any interest in or need to try skateboarding. It seemed redundant: I was always already indulging in plenty of other opportunities for injury and death. Besides, I didn't hang around with anyone who skateboarded. But about ten years ago I fell in with this group of guys whom I seemed to have a lot in common with – fellow backcountry skiers, river runners and new parents – except for one peculiar trait: on autumn full-moon nights, they would bring their surfer backgrounds home to Colorado by taking ritualistic longboard rides down our region's highway mountain passes.

These tales always sounded insane to me, of course. And it took a decade of befuddlement in the face of their sick stories before I felt, for the first time, that I should at least sample what these otherwise intelligent people found so appealing in this modern madness for going really fast down paved hills on wooden slats attached to little wheels.

Webb was also an inspiration. He is a skateboarding whiz – a regular riding, gliding, jumping, ollying, kick-flipping, sliding and grinding skateboarding stud. His impressive skill came from only one thing: practicing, on his own, a lot – because where ever Webb is, there he trains. When I commented on this clever use of time and space once last year, he surprised me with an innocuous, yet wise, insight: "Two minutes skateboarding is a good two minutes," he waxed philosophically. So he whips it out … where ever. When we get gas, he's grinding the curb around the gas pumps. If we have to run into a store, he's surfing the fall lines of the parking lot. Last year, when we spent a few days at a condo complex at a ski resort, he was nearly as excited by the subterranean terrain of the parking garage as he was the mountain. "When I see something like that, I can't resist," he explained.

Pretty cool stuff. And enlightening: seen through Webb's skateboarding eyes, even the most developed of spaces revert to wild places – meaningful, rich in depth and texture, full of purpose and value, and ripe with potential for exploration. And I started to think that, as Webb and I sink deeper into his wild teen-age adventure together – which I'd like to do with Webb as more of a friend than a father, doing more sharing than shaping – maybe it's time I entered his world for a change. And maybe skateboarding could be that doorway.

So that's how I ended up here tonight, standing at the tippety toppest of the highest paved hill in Durango, facing a mile-long run in the dark down to the first run-out. Which will be just the launching point for the next run. And so on. For many runs. It's not the hairpin turns and sheer drop-offs to bone-crunching boulder fields of a, say, Coal Bank Pass. But for a first rite of passage, it seems dumb enough.

When I hatched my plan to enter into skateboarding, I opted for the longboard route. It not only bridged me to my older boarding buddies, it also seemed more suited to my backcountry-skiing sensibilities.

I soon found that the skill of longboarding itself isn't hard. It was awkward at first: I had never surfed or snowboarded, so the whole standing-sideways thing felt unnatural and unwise for my telemarking and karate-trained body, both sports in which you get low and face your foe. But the theory common to all sports soon fit in: control your center, bend your knees, keep your upper body quiet. The real trick to my survival at first, though, was to stay at speeds where I could resort to the jump-and-run method of self-arrest. I even deliberately at first wore no helmet or padding to be sure I stayed within my limits, to remove the temptation to let it rip too soon.

To let it rip, though, I needed to really carve. So I sought out some pointers from my experienced companions. Funny thing is, nobody could tell me anything. "Just … go" was what everyone seemed to mumble, shrugging their collective shoulders. So I eventually forged my own tele-karate-skateboard form that my body could work with, and soon I could fly (it felt to me) down entire multi-block-long pitches in my neighborhood, getting long, loose runs that let me improve my stiff swaying and nervous swerving into somewhat confident – and increasingly speed-controlling – carves.

And once that happened, it was time to venture farther afield. It was my turn to just go.

I watch my companions push off, one by one, each picking up speed before leaning and carving – I can't help but make the comparison – lovely backcountry-skiing quality S-turns down the hardpan fall line, until they fade into the now-moonless gloom.

My turn. I push off and assume my personal "just go" position, then start making the hard turns I need to to keep my velocity tempered. This first run isn't steep, but it's steep enough. And long – that's the clincher. Even though this time I'm wearing a helmet and wrist guards, I make a vow that I'm not going too far over my head – as much as I'm enjoying longboarding, there's other things I'd rather die doing. And when I feel that point approaching where my speed is exceeding my maximum-runnable-velocity, I leap and sprint to a stop, and start over.

The problem, of course, is the pavement. Or, more accurately, my own intense awareness of that pavement rapidly scrolling by only a few inches under my feet. Gravity can work quickly or slowly, but given enough slope, it's gonna work. So even on a relatively gentle but non-stop hill like this, it doesn't take long for the Second Law of Skateboarding Thermodynamics to kick in: Once you pass the point of jumping-and-running, there's no natural force other than friction that is going to transform your moving body into a body at rest. You just hope that friction comes in the benign form of hard carves and, ultimately, a gentle run-out that leads to stoppage.

That, right there, is the aspect of skateboarding distinguishing it from other sports: fall and you are guaranteed to pay with the proverbial – and literal – pound of flesh. No way around it. And that absolutism is the way you have to go into longboarding in particular: *I will not fall*. So that line where you know you cannot leap off and survive is like a psychological sound barrier – you can almost feel the psychic sonic-boom in your intestines as you pass through that panting, near-panic phase where the primordial fight/flee debate becomes irrelevant and you emerge into that raw oh-shit-just-hang-on territory. Or, if you can abandon to that, this becomes that magical no-think-just-perform realm.

But, really, isn't this the point? Isn't that what we're seeking in all our extreme sports, or anything challenging? Abandon. And particularly, the willingness to abandon in the face of some seriously risky exposure. That's also the power – hell, the sorcery – revealed and bequeathed in these acts, whether it's on a rock face, a steep snowy slope, a rocky stretch of single-track, or even in front of an audience or classroom or workplace presentation – abandon in the face of some difficult exposure. And to do it well – with skill and style and even beauty – is what we call grace.

Tonight, the exposure is in a dose way beyond what I'd faced thus far in my month-long apprenticeship. And the abandon? It's coming … slowly, but definitely coming, as I squat lower on the board (that telemarking/karate thing again) and lean harder into the turns. Grace is perhaps a ways away, but still something good is happening: Houses and driveways approach – faster and faster – and pass. The pavement becomes a wave across whose face I sweep back and forth rather than frightfully bulleting straight down. And as my technique grows more and more assertive, I'm finding that my board responds as it should to my improving, increasing abandon by keeping my speed scary but sane.

As I emerge into the streetlight-lit flat section of roadway that marks the end of this first epic downhill mile, my board rolls to a smoothly slowing stop. As my comrades-in-abandon greet me with high-fives and hoots, it strikes me that there just might be something even yet deeper to this skateboarding thing.

The next pitch takes us down another dark neighborhood. It's near midnight now, so there's little traffic. And I'm feeling good – I'm getting low, attacking turns, riding across the face of the road in sharp switchbacks, leaning hard into the right handers and bravely hanging my ass – protected only by a single layer of blue jean – over the road on the lefties.

There's something to be said about this.

Beyond the skill, apart from the camaraderie, aside from the inherent rewards of getting low and facing the foe of our primordial fear of head-cracking and flesh-smearing, there is one thing longboarding has given me that I truly didn't expect: the world. I mean the world that I thought had been already lost to concrete and construction and the generally urban/suburban pox on the land that I, being one of those weepy, hillbilly, enviro-meddler sorts, general flees from and avoids.

And in these past few weeks, I found, through this mini-wheeled medium, landscapes – entire worlds full of detail and subtlety and challenge and even unique beauty – right at the end of my front walk. Right down the street – past the funky little steep alley, in the summer lined with feral sunflowers, that can give you a quick launch in three different directions. Right through the intersection with a different kind of tree on each corner – juniper, cottonwood, silver maple, and box elder. Up the block with the yellow-plum trees. To where the road rises above town in an anomalous little steep-sided neighborhood with tall, thin houses – and where there's the post-card-quality view through a stand of blue spruces of the long line of the La Platas bursting above the foothills on the west side of town

Something was coming alive as I looked around from the deck of my longboard.

Once I could ride those runs through town with some skill and that blooming enjoyment, my companions and I decided it was time for some forays afield. That's how we started exploring the subdivisions carved into so many of the foothill valleys around here.

When we could, we would – like on any powder day – gather in the morning with coffee and our boards and fill a car to capacity to drive to some development that had struck someone's curiosity or fancy or sense of challenge. And we'd enter it like we would any valley that we were approaching with backcountry gear: with a mental topographic mapping of the curves and rolls and pitches and fall lines of the land, and with a wider eye toward the grander forest setting and mountain backdrop and patterns of drainage. Then we would spend hours riding those places – places that became places for the first time to my backcountry-roaming eyes. Through those wild-seeking eyes.

And when we rode – a pack of us hooting and working hard and roaming around, then walking those long earn-your-turn jaunts back up those routes just run – I found the very things I'd always left town to find.

Here's what I find tonight: the warm yellow lights, like golden pools marking the crossings in the town's gridwork, interspersed with dark swaths of mystery and potential danger. The damp air rich, full of the scents of sage and soil and wet pavement. The chill of the misty drizzle on my face. The only sound the low roll and echo of my compatriots' wheels as they snake away in and out of the patches of light.

It ain't wilderness, but it is wild.

It's worth mentioning, by the way, that like most things good and cheap and liberating and intoxicating, this making domesticated landscapes wild again isn't legal. "Skateboarding is not a crime," skateboarders love to proclaim; but, alas, Colorado State Statute 42-4-109 states otherwise:

> No person shall use the highways for traveling on skis, toboggans, coasting sleds, skates, or similar devices. It is unlawful for any person to use any roadway of this state as a sled or ski course for the purpose of coasting on sleds, skis, or similar devices.

This is, of course, absurd.

Aside from the myriad spiritual and philosophical and physical rewards cited above, the skateboard is also eminently pragmatic, as I see every day walking around both town and college campus, where for many people the skateboard functions as a cheap, portable, and eminently effective means of transportation. Hummers should be the crime before skateboards.

Since skateboards are of little harm to anyone but those willing to risk them, we can see, perhaps, a prejudice behind skateboarding's being a crime. I cite as an example one of our own city councilors, who, when Durango was seeking to approve a new downtown skate park, sounded like the elected representative of the Flat Earth Society when he said that if it were built it would need "a full-time security guard" armed with "a police radio." Stating his intention to oppose the project, he added: "Anyone that thinks the park will be a healthy outlet for children probably still believes in the tooth fairy."

Absurd. When my family and I spent two months last summer driving from Durango to Alaska and back, we looked for lots of cool things: lakes and mountains, towns and wildlife, hikes and fishing spots. And we looked for skateboard parks. As we approached towns, even on remote stretches of the Alaska highway, we could refer to our travel guides and find towns that boasted their skateboard parks. Those are the towns we chose to stay in. At first, we stopped just because we knew Webb and Anna could use the break and exercise; but we soon were surprised to find that by taking our kids to these skateparks – wonderful, huge, creative creations, and all free of charge – we also got to meet some great people. Young people. Teenagers.

In particular I remember Haines, Alaska. Sitting at the end of a highway in the southeastern part of the state, the town recently built a beautiful year-round sheltered skateboard park – which the town's teens were actively involved in both designing and maintaining. The kids we talked to were clearly proud of their park and their involvement in making it happen. We ended up turning our planned quick-visit to Haines into a week-long stay in no small part because we felt safe enough to let Webb venture there on his own to hang with his new acquaintances – an experience he still describes as some of his most treasured on our trip.

A tribe, I tell you. Yet another organic connection rising like a weed and rooted in sharing something powerful, legal or not.

And they're everywhere. I mean my friends here, of course, but I also mean the old doctor we found walking his dog on one of our subdivision expeditions, who stopped us – we expected a scolding and eviction – to reminisce with us for half an hour about surfing and taking his kids out to skateboard the aqueducts in California. Like the woman who stopped her minivan to share her excitement over her and her family's having just scored a bunch of longboards cheap off eBay. Like the 10-year-old who stopped and sat on his skateboard to watch us padded-up old-timers riding through town, giving us high fives as we rolled by. When Jan and I went back up after and asked him for any pointers he might have, he shrugged and said, "Just go."

Of course. Because that's what this tribe does.

By the time we arrive near the river, it's raining pretty good. But we're feeling it now, and even Jan and I are riding some slides in our hard carves. I finish my run with a face shot in a deep puddle that I part with a big wake.

This old dog likes his new trick.

Why am I doing this? It's not, I can assure you, to "be young," or "recapture my youth." I don't need to recapture my youth: It's right here. It's in my vow that even if I die old, broken, blind, and decrepit, I'm going to die young. And tomorrow morning, when I gulp coffee and babble excitedly to Webb about this night and my new-found skateboarding enlightenment, he's going to shake his head solemnly and say, "Dad, I been telling ya ..."

I'll promise to listen more.

He is not with us tonight, though. It being the middle of a school night and we being out breaking the law and all. But the next full moon is on a weekend, and I think it's time we take on one of those mountain passes, together.

But tonight's not done yet. While we stand around yakking under a street light in the middle of the night, a Durango cop car approaches. Its inhabitants are invisible in the night, but I can feel their skeptical scrutinizing. Until, that is, either the gray hairs or our middle-age full-body armor overrides any alarm the skateboards might have raised. The cruiser slows, but rolls on by.

After it passes, somebody suggests a route back toward home. It's a bit roundabout, but it has some runs he'd been eyeing lately. All agree. The morning is young, and so are we.

We push off in a pack, like a pack of old dogs, and just go.

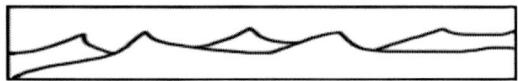

Writer Without a Cause

For several years now, I've been writing a column about living and loving and roaming in the Four Corners area. Recently I was asked by some of that column's regular readers (both of them, actually) what it is I'm getting at in those dispatches.

This isn't unusual – I'm used to readers who aren't shy about speaking back. Bless them. In this case, though, they were referring to an uncertainty about what, exactly, is the philosophy I spout in that column. That, I decided, was a good question, because I couldn't come up with an answer. What is my "philosophy"? Well … I dunno. And as someone who can't help but try to put things into words – every damned thing it seems sometimes – I was surprised to realize that even I didn't know how to label my work and words.

So I gave myself the task of roping that rambling perspective. And so I spent some time sifting through a stack of those columns, seeking threads, stalking common themes, keeping an eye out for recurring thoughts and tracking traces of rationality, reason, direction, definition, or principle.

Through that reviewing, I was surprised to find myself to be a writer who, having to write about something for every issue of a magazine, has written about damned near everything at one point or another. I dug through stories I'd crafted about river running, walking barefoot, rolling in the mud with kids, sleeping out in my backyard, smoking cigars, celebrating spring, getting drunk in dive bars, fighting for public lands, fighting against the Animas-La Plata Project, playing baseball, bow hunting, bass fishing, powder skiing, doing nothing at all, my crazy friends, my warrior wife, Merle Haggard, the small-mountain-town tribe, and … you get the idea. Assuming there's an idea to get.

As I sifted and sorted those heaps of sentences and paragraphs, though, I was, more than anything, surprised to find that what bound that broad spectrum of rants and reflections together was … absolutely nothing.

And then it hit me: My gods, I don't have a philosophy!

This was dismaying. I mean, what kind of writer am I? What do I say next time I'm in my favorite neighborhood bar and some fellow patron I meet asks what I do (which is how we identify ourselves, no?), and I say, with an affected air like Hemingway, that I'm a writer. And then he or she asks, well, what do I write about? Following would be an awkward pause. Some quiet, solitary sips. Then the end of the conversation. Then I'd be stuck alone at the bar, again, like the poor, lonely factory slob in one of those Merle Haggard songs I wrote about.

I grew frantic. There must be some label under which I can brand my body of work. Surely some pop-philosophy term must fit: simplicity … environmentalism … nature writing … hillbilly Buddhism … radical environmental parenting … Paleolithic travelogue … anything. Something. But, no: Nothing seemed to describe the direction in which my writing blows. Regardless, as other fans have kindly pointed out, my writing does nonetheless often blow.

And it also often has a direction. Label or not, I can look at my own life and see that I'm headed down some sort of distinct, albeit little-traveled, path. Something is leading me to do such irregular things, in both my life and my writing, with such regularity.

It came to me, appropriately enough, in a moment of sparkling insight while doing one of those irregular things – in this case, meditating upon a full moon as I hung out in yet another doomed wild place, sitting in the cold night under a Utah juniper bearing a remarkable resemblance to a Bodhi tree. It was there that I finally understood myself, that I at last saw inside and straight through my spirit, that I once and for all reached the lip of the cliff at the end of my search for personal meaning, and when I looked over I saw … nothing. Again.

And then I realized The Truth at last: My philosophy is No Philosophy.

And that's what I see in my collected works: no philosophy, no plan, no program, no map. I just write how I live: Here. Now. What's in my face. What's in my line of sight. What's burning at the candle-flame-tip of my heart and soul at the moment.

And then wandering merrily on to the next here-and-now – not following a path, but leaving a trail, largely of words, with writings like cairns, saying to fellow travelers, Hey! Here's something cool!

And it dawned on me that I like it that way. I don't *want* a philosophy.

That, folks, *is* my philosophy.

The fact is, I don't want to know how to live – or, worse, I don't want to think I know how to live. I also don't want to be told how to live. And I sure as hell don't want to pretend to tell others how to live. I just want to live.

Really, that's it.

And that's really all I write about: what happened to me while I was being alive.

This, though, did not solve my initial challenge: to label what I do. The Buddhists, of course, already have a term for this: Mindfulness. Mindfulness is … just being in the moment … being in your being … being the moment … being in your being in the moment in any situation, perceiving without judgment or evaluation or assigning meaning or value, or plotting or planning, or … anything. It's just taking it all in.

It's sounds simple, and it is … but it isn't so simple, is it? Because it certainly goes against our training and conditioning. And it begins in school – which is like anti-mindfulness practice. School takes the feral little mammals that kids are and stuffs them into great big boxes for six or eight hours a day, making them sit still, do what they're told, focus on thinking thinking thinking, then demanding they change their focus on-command at the sound of the bell. Quit playing around! Keep quiet! Stay in line! Keep your hands to yourself! What's your problem? Why aren't you enjoying this?!?

The moment? The senses? The sensual and stimulating presence in a living, dynamic, ever-changing, ever-challenging great big world? Well, if they're lucky, the kids get to read about that. Or run frantically through it at recess, or for an hour or two before homework, dinner, chores, and bed.

And why do we put our kids through this? Because they need that training in order to survive the monotony, routine, sensual deprivation, and mental occupation when they're big mammals toiling diligently inside the office or factory or garage or warehouse for forty or sixty hours a week, before they go drive home to their home-entertainment centers and chore-filled houses. They need the discipline so they won't question the program when their daily lives lapse into an unbroken string of years punctuated only by the bestowed gifts of weekends off, and the granted allotments of two or three weeks of vacation a year, during which times they'll work hard finding that buried, nagging, vague aching for something akin to mindfulness, but for which their minds will be much too full to be mindful.

Okay, excuse the snarl.

See, that's why even though I like the language of Buddhism, I'm a lousy Buddhist. Because even if I like the symbolism and rhetoric of Buddhism, I have one argument with Buddha: I believe circumstances matter. Buddhism would tell me, Chill! Transcend the conditions of our time, Grasshopper! The goal of Buddhism is to achieve mindfulness regardless of circumstances or situations, through discipline and training and practice, because to be mindful is to desire nothing other than what is. "Desire only desirelessness," Buddha advised.

Well, I think that's a noble endeavor and a fine goal. But I just ain't that patient. Or maybe I don't have that gift of endurance. Either way, I'm no where near "enlightened." So, with all due respect to The Buddha, I myself don't desire desirelessness – I desire to desire deliberately.

So while good Buddhists are sitting on their cushions silently meditating their way to mindfulness, I can't help but be off again, somewhere, out there, with no plan, program, philosophy, or guiding ideas, hunting situations to feed my mind a full serving of life, regularly desiring irregular things, seeking crazy situations, stalking wild people, actively rather than passively in search of my own sort of hillbilly-guy-out-doing-things kind of Buddhism.

Not mindfulness, but *mindfillingness.*

And, since I'm that person who can't help put things into words, that which has filled my mind has ended up in my columns, in my writing, in my books.

Thanks for asking.

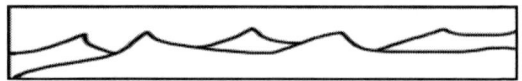

Just Say Yes, Yes, YES!

*I*t's late. Or early, depending upon your frame of reference. From Mark's frame of reference, it's late. He sleeps in the chair next to me, his head resting on his chin, which rests on his chest. From the frame of reference of our trip as a whole, though, it's early, given that we still have two more full days ahead of us on the river.

Early it is, then, I decree. To toast this decision, I take Mark's beer from his limp hand and finish it for him. What are friends for?

There's no shame in Mark's dozing, even though around him our entire boating party parties on with typical shameless male debauchery – campfire, beer, shots, cigars. Guitars ring out Neil Young tunes, old friends catch up missed months, occasional barbaric yawps launch into the moonlight. We've earned our festivity, and Mark has earned his slumber. We had a big evening on the San Juan River – a night of paddling, which is a big change from our daily routines. And change is tiring.

We had put on the river late in the afternoon. It's November, so the sun sets early, but we had miles to go before we sleep. We were counting on the moon: It's between first quarter and full, so we knew it'd already be high at sunset, and giving off a fair share of lumens.

We were right. For the first hour we paddled into and under a long, drawn-out sunset full of luminescent pastels that I didn't know existed, and some I never thought could exist. But there they were, slipping into semi-darkness, then finally succumbing to the light of the nearly full moon. And then everything changed again. Think about it: We perceive the world we live in, the landscape around us, mostly by sight and light – meaning sunlight. So this landscape navigated under light from a different source is a different perception, meaning it is a different landscape.

Other things have changed, too. The river itself, in particular. In August, the corner of Dinetah, the Navajo Nation, on the south side of the river was declared a disaster area for drought. In September, though, the river spiked up to 16,000 c.f.s. under massive rains from marauding thunderstorms. Again this part of the Navajo Reservation was declared a disaster area, but this time for floods.

The effects of that radical change are obvious: new sandbars where before was flatwater, wide spots channelized into tight little swiftwater runs, and unexpected new branches leading into braided mazes. I thought I knew this river well, but my old mental maps and expectations had to be immediately 86ed under the dull, black-light-like moonglow. So I relearn the river, stroke by stroke, poco a poco.

Ah, well, nothing "wrong" or malicious in these changes. It's just the nature of this powerful land, this lovely river, this single blessed night. Good for us, then, since change is why we're out here. We're here to experience something totally different. Different from what? The daily world. The daily program. The evening TV programs. The years or decades (barring early unplanned fatal change) of life's program ahead. You know. The usual.

So that's how we got here. And that's why Mark is tired and the rest of us wired, early into and late the first night of the Annual San Juan River Men's Trip.

And all I can think of adding is to lift Mark's beer to the moonlit night and say: Yes.

Back on the river. We float on, three canoes and a duckie, seven middle-aged men (okay, four middle-aged men and three who are going to be soon enough) out on a Stone Age mission: Isn't this just an early 21st Century version of the monthly or semi-monthly hunting party? Think of the variety that the required ritual of having to regularly hunt some large mammals injected into people's lives. Going out for a mammoth or bison or kudu or whale wasn't just men out on poker night – these forays had real, life-or-death consequences, for both the participants and for those waiting for the meat and leather. For all involved, these trips had sacred meaning – adventure, mystery, power, camaraderie, and challenge, all infused on a regular basis into men's lives, and the lives of the women whose immense responsibility it was to maintain, defend, and run the village or camp. And it had meaning for the kids who knew they would soon assume those roles.

Once or twice a month was guaranteed change – unpredictable, unplannable, unavoidable.

And since those hunting forays have been part of our lives for 99/100s of our time as human beings, it makes sense, in my simple hillbilly logic, that the aching for this regular routine-jolting change is still genetically lodged in us. Our problem is trying to work it into our modern prescripted lives.

"Well, it's not the only problem, but it's a big one, don't you think?" I conclude my sermon.

Scott and Dave, paddling in the boat alongside us, mull this over. Mark agrees. "Fucking right," he concurs from the bow of our boat.

"Maybe," Scott says. "But there's this guy who's trying to burn as few calories as possible. He tries to eat only a little, and move hardly at all. He thinks he'll live longer if he doesn't use up his body. He calls himself 'a living experiment.'"

None of us knows quite what to say to that. We pass the mouth of Chinle Wash, which in September must have been a major river. Now it is a thin ribbon of flatwater meandering away toward some pale distant bluffs. Looking downstream I can see the mouth of the canyon cut into the redrock chevrons marking the rise of the Lime Ridge Anticline. I wonder what changes will be waiting down in the canyon. I wonder what Eight Foot Rapid will look like.

"I guess I'd rather use up my body," Dave finally answers.

"Fucking right!" Mark agrees.

Down into the canyon. Float, rapids, float, rapids, float … lots of familiar stuff. And lots of changes – rearranged boulder fields, new whitewater slots, random sandbars. We reach Eight Foot Rapid just before dusk. The rapid lies around the vertical edge of a cliff, but as we paddle close to the turn we can hear it hissing and grumbling.

Even though I last ran this only a few months ago, we don't know the football-field-long stretch of whitewater may have been rearranged by September's deluges. We turn the canoe to an angle across the current so when we come around the canyon wall we have our best chance of quickly responding to whatever lies beyond.

There's a great difference between running a rapid you know well and reading a river while running it. And Eight Foot ain't what I remember – it's been channeled on the right by new rubble, and several boulders have been tossed into the main line to make things more interesting than they already were. We work the boat hard, but although we take on some water, we have no problems. We paddle hard at the bottom of the rapid to the beach on river left.

After us, everyone has good runs, and soon we're together and in grand spirits setting up our night's camp. Eric does some kind of primitive dance in the sand under his sombrero. Matt jumps into preparing cocktails. Randall lights a fire. Within an hour, the guitars come out again, cocktails splash out of tin cups, raw hunks of elk sizzle over the fire.

Sometime later, Mark and I stand on the shore of the river smoking cheap cigars, watching the moon bubble up over the canyon rim and not saying anything in the sacred moment. Until I offer one word:

Yes!

It's morning, but late enough for the November sun to have risen above the rust-red canyon wall across the river. I sit under a ledge above camp. Below me, my comrades play cards. Beyond them lies the river, a dirty-white conveyor through an asteroid belt of boulders. The rumbles and hisses echo off the cliff.

I ought to be meditating or something, I guess. But I guess that even though I've been studying Buddhism for two decades now, I'm just too redneck to be a good cushion-sitting meditator. I'm more bubba than Buddha. Rather than "original mind" – the goal of Zen practice – I'm busy looking for my "savage" mind. So rather than sitting, I tend to paddle, hike, ski, wander, run, spar, drink beer, and "hunt" on men's trips as my meditation.

But does that really make me that far off track? After all, isn't the goal of Zen – a mind that is alert, aware, present, living with what just is and rolling with change – just the re-creation of the hunter's mind through will and training? And if that's so, can't it be that that state of mind is genetically encoded – some kind of Pleistocene Dharma that we are still called to follow, even though we live in a culture that encourages over-thinking, mega-routine, predictable expectation, safety and security and things like living longer by not using up the body?

This, then, leads to my hillbilly divergence with traditional Buddhism: if we're craving that mind, doesn't it make sense to get our asses up off that cushion and back into the circumstances that require that mind?

On that note, I crawl down from my perch, wander past my coffee-drinking river-rat friends, head up the beach and crawl over some blocks of sandstone the size of Volkswagens. Past the boulder field, I stumble into the midst of a herd of two dozen or so big horn sheep. I bow politely, apologize, angle off to the right. I arrive at a secluded little beach dotted with dainty big horn tracks. There, I meditate, my way: I pull off all my clothes, then walk out and slide into the icy late-fall river.

YES!

Next day, more men's trippiness: slow floats … a quick rip through Ledge Rapid … a long stop for nine innings of sandbar baseball … then, we exit the canyon and paddle on into dusk, as the moon gleams overhead and the setting autumn sun sets the bluffs aflame, as cool November air flows down the canyon. We're tired from all the changes we've experienced, but we're in no hurry, because the end of this trip means our return to the "real world" – a world that resists change.

And I wonder, as I do at the end of every one of these so blessed, too-infrequent forays into the real real world: how do I take this back with me?

Take back what? I've come to realize that my obsession with getting out on the river, out on adventures, and out with my men friends is not just to be away from civilized life, as much as I might sincerely like to unmake civilization. Since I can't, though, my obsession is this: I want to know how it felt to live wildly. Even in my sometimes mundane world of job and house and bills, I desperately want to know what it meant to see the world that way.

And when I seek that compass bearing, that sensibility, that "original mind," the mind of the hunter, the gatherer, the forager, the warrior, I keep coming up with only one word: Yes.

JUST SAY YES, YES, YES!

And I realize, that's it: the thing I really want in my life, always, every day, to my moment of death ... I want my dying words to be: Yes! *Yes!* YES!

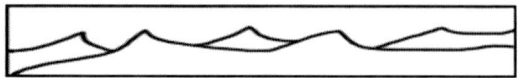

Unhandy Man

hen I was a kid, I thought my dad could do it all. I wasn't far off, since he could do most of it: he was the consummate jack-of-all-trades, a regular redneck Renaissance man – he could tear down a motorcycle engine to its elemental parts then reassemble it; he bought several old houses, in which he then spent years' worth of nights gutting and rebuilding, doing the carpentry, plumbing, and much of the wiring himself; he was a hunter, fisherman, woodsman, and champion archer; he drew, painted, and whittled statuettes of old fishermen with a pocketknife; and he read voraciously, shaping himself into a self-taught historian on our New England homeland.

As a kid, I was, of course, ever his pupil and apprentice. I learned to repair my own motorcycle, to wield power tools, to eat off the land – "If you ever get lost, I expect to find you fatter than when you left," he'd admonish – and to appreciate the history in the towns and landscape around us. And even though I've since traded my Suzuki for a bicycle, bow for skis, hammer for laptop, paints for words, and the Appalachians for the Rockies, I to this day maintain a warm and deep gratitude for the many skills he imparted to me. I also know that that act of passing on those skills sealed a sacred exchange fathers and mothers have shared with their children for thousands of millennia.

Along with an appreciation for that experience, though, and magnified by that sense of primordial parental duty, here in my own middle age and with my own kids, I find that I also carry a keen awareness of the shortcomings in my own skill-imparting skills.

I know this is largely due simply to the differences in my and my father's personalities. Also, though, part of my inadequacy stems from our disparate life paths. My dad had a kid when he was young, and so had to sharpen his skills at skill-learning in order to build a life from the ground up. I, on the other hand, chose to head out across that ground rather than to stay and build on it. So I've spent my adult life traveling. And in that traveling life, those technical skills I learned as a teen have slowly degraded and faded from lack of practice – or, as I prefer to see it, were exchanged for seeing lots of places, for meeting many people, for being outside as much as possible, and for working (as little as possible) at a lot of odd jobs to get by.

This includes the years I've spent ostensibly "settled down" – but really still traveling, just more deeply than widely – in my adopted homeland, here in the Four Corners country. Which is how, I suppose, I got here today.

It is a lovely Saturday morning, and I and a couple of friends are climbing up a gleaming slope high in the San Juans. We have skins on our skis, avalanche beacons on our bodies, and packs on our backs stuffed with things like extra layers of clothing, collapsible shovels, summer sausage and cheese and bottles of water. We climb to the base of a broad band of silvery grey limestone bluffs, drop our packs, unleash our skis, and sit, the angled snow conforming to the shapes of our tired, happy bodies.

There on that snowy slope, with the high-altitude winter sun sending a searing light ricocheting around the high-country basin, my fellow middle-aged ski/river/mountain/desert bums and I pass around chunks of cheddar and processed meat products. And we stare – just sit and silently stare, for a long time – at the ragged wintery glory all around us.

This, I have come to find in the middle of my life, is what I do. This, and float on rivers. And run down trails. And hike up canyons. And paddle across lakes. And sleep outside of walls every chance I get. And spend time with a lot of really good people – as many as I can – who like to do that kind of stuff.

That's it, really. That is what I do.

And that realization is somewhat unsettling. For as the window of opportunity slowly – although less slowly by the year, the week, the day – passes for me to be that skill-bearing parental figure my father was, I am taken aback and little embarrassed to find that I possess few real mechanical, artistic, pragmatic, or trade-worthy skills to spend my evenings bestowing upon my two young adolescent acolytes. Because of my choice to focus my life on just getting out and experiencing the world, it appears I have become an unskilled laborer. A jack of no trades.

What am I good at? Well, I'm good at this. What I'm doing now, here on this mountainside. I'm good at savoring. At presence. I'm good at actually getting out – and at finding lovely, dramatic, powerful places to get out into.

Taking note of the fine friends who have joined me today, I'll say I'm good at surrounding myself with caring, thoughtful, happy, fun, and active people.

More? Looking back at the wandering, wayfaring life I've lived thus far – and see no immediate end to – I'd say I'm good at enjoying my days and letting go of most of my worries. Almost to a fault some might say, but so be it – because I'm also good at having faith in the flow of the world. And in that flow, I seem to be pretty good at adapting to ever-changing circumstances and doing whatever it takes to get through. (Hence my "career" vita of a multitude of mundane and multifaceted jobs, my dearth of savings, and my lack of retirement plan.)

Most of all, though, I hope I'm good at being a father and husband and member of a meaningful, rooted community – that "traveling deeply" thing.

Note in that list, though, no specific and practical skills that a father and son or daughter can work on together in the garage or in the back yard or around the woodstove at night.

Still, I wonder. Can exploring the world be a skill? How about loving to use your body? Just being present? Can exploring and knowing and savoring a place be a skill? Being a good friend, lover, or elder? How about simply enjoying life?

Could, perhaps, those things – place, tribe, even your self, and even living itself – be turned from nouns into verbs? Into activities? Into studyable, improvable, communicatable skills?

Lunch done, we rise from our frozen recliners and set about preparing to descend: strip and stow away skins, repack packs, check beacons, click into skis. Then one of my companions is off, diving down the uncut slope spilling out below us, his body riding the glide of his curving, carving skis. Then my other friend drops, and I watch him, too, as he dances with his descent down the mountain.

Before I join them, I pause for a moment. A long, deep, tangible, tactile moment in which I am just there – just there as good as I can be just there. Better than the last time I was just somewhere.

But not as good as I'll endeavor to be there the next time I'm just somewhere.

And right then I realize that if skills like this are practicable, then perhaps they are, after all, also teachable. If so, then they'll have to be "taught" the way my father taught me how to hunt, to tear down an engine, to draw, and to study my place: not through any plan, program or curriculum, but by just doing them, and by doing them together, regardless of where that doing takes place.

Because doing itself may be the best skill of all.

Excellent
Adventures

It's what you do that makes your soul,
not the other way around.
Barbara Kingsolver

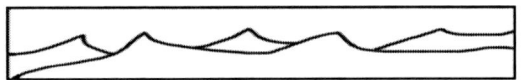

Webb and Anna's Excellent Adventure

*I*t was time to roll. Roll down the river. Roll like the river. It was time to river trip, or something like it.

The day after the kids got out of school, we loaded our old van and headed out, Webb and Anna and I, while Sarah was home using the time alone preparing for a real river trip. This seemed an appropriate day to hit the road, it being the start of summer for the kids – "summer" as a way of living (no school!) rather than a season, per se. And so this trip is for Webb and Anna – being a good, concerned parent, I wanted to take them out and debrief them, decompress them, give them a ceremony to bring them out of the Cultural Training Program that is school and back into the Real World Out There. A purification before the lazy, crazy daze of summer, when kids get to again be kids, until their training resumes in August.

And there's nothing like a river trip for that. Or river-style trip, anyway.

In lieu of actual river running, though, for this trip we would be driving alongside a river. But it would be river-trip-like: We would cover a short distance over a long period of time. No plan. No schedule. No agenda. Just three days driving and camping and playing, the river our constant companion. The only potential dark cloud in the bright sky of our excellent adventure was that this was Memorial Day Weekend, and on this weekend, most of the Four Corners is surrendered to the tourist hordes that help pay for our lovely lifestyle. So the kids and I opted to go where there aren't going to be many tourists. Where there is no shopping, pavement, lodging, entertainment, phones, TVs, bars …

Where's that? … well, no matter. Suffice to say that where we go is lovely, even without those conveniences: a major stream flanked by a good-enough gravel road. An old railroad bed winds along the winding river, too, offering some exploring opportunities, with even a couple of abandoned railroad towns thrown in. We are "headed out," as Neil Young sings, "to where the pavement turns to sand."

On this route, the pavement turns to sand where the river rolls through some sandy, p-j covered hills, sparsely populated by old houses that look like they belong here, like they were built to be lived in rather than just visited, built as homes rather than trophies. The drive is pleasant, the old van humming smoothly, swinging with the swings in the river road like a big canoe.

But we can only drive so long before we must get out, and so we soon pull up to a gravel turnout along the river. The kids are ready, ecstatic, and so am I. We climb out of the van into the hot, dry air of summer.

The river here is a wide, dirty, swollen flow. The kids run down to the grassy bench under sweeping narrowleaf cottonwoods, while I eye the old railroad route along the riverside, offering an inviting trail through tamarisk stands. A great spot. And simple: just a dirt lot with absolutely no amenities. This is plenty good, the kids decide. And it's their adventure, so we stay. I drag a chair and a book down to the grassy riverside while Webb and Anna wander and play – with no toys or gadgets or the aid of the Disney Corporation, just completely content with just the place and the "toys" provided on site.

No curriculum.

Just this.

After a few hours of doing nothing, I ask the kids if they want to roll on, mosey on down to the ghost town down the road, or to just see what other spot along the river we can find to camp, just for something to do. But they want to camp here.

The only trouble is, you're not supposed to camp here.

The land around this stream and in the hills is mostly public, managed by a variety of agencies (depending upon which side of imaginary boundaries you happen to find yourself on), and checkerboarded by tracts of private land. Only one of these public-land management agencies allows random camping, though. And the problem is, where we are right now is managed by one of those less-accommodating agencies.

I have to come out of the closet here, though: I'm am a notorious camping poacher. It started when I was a kid: Even growing up in thickly settled southern New England, I instinctively understood, long before I read about Zapata, what he meant when he argued, "The land, like the air we breathe, belongs to everyone, and to no one." So I have to admit it: camping illegally has been a favorite game since I was young. Back then, friends and/or I would sneak out to sleep out somewhere, anywhere – in other friends' back yards, in unsuspecting neighbors' woods, or where ever we wanted along the shore of the all-private lake I lived on. In the morning we (or I alone) would sneak back from where ever we bedded down, fully charged and excited by both the freedom and the risk.

Oddly, I never quite outgrew this primordial impulse to treat the world as my very own. In college in New Hampshire, I would drag my amazed friends out into the nearby College Woods for nights out under the stars. Then, after college, when I was out on the road, I would find all kinds of side streets and hidden roads and empty parking lots to carry out my car-hobo ways. Even as a supposedly more mature graduate student living in downtown metro Boulder, Colorado, I would frequently, on a complete whim, stuff a sleeping bag into a little backpack and wander up into the foothills in the Boulder Mountain Park – where, even in The People's Republic of Boulder, camping is strictly verboten! – to spend a lovely night with the celestial stars above and city stars below.

I have even carried this hobby abroad: I'm proud to say I've camped illegally hidden in hedgerows in little Swiss mountain villages, on park benches in rural Germany, and in any number of other places as close as Canada and as far away as Africa. On these travels, I even found kindred countries out there: In Scandinavia, a wayfarer such as I can camp legally damn near anywhere. It's called "Allemansret," or "Everyman's Right," an ancient law that pre-dates the Vikings that allows people to camp on private or public land, guided only by a few rules of basic respect.

Here in the good ol' US of A, though – home of the free and land of the fee – we have retained the ancestral right to cross open country only in a few limited public places, and even then usually under strict rules and for fees. But that hasn't stopped me, for I'm a firm believer in human rights – humans as animals in the world rather than merely citizens in some country. So, thinking about all that after my kids asked me to camp here, I think … why not raise my kids right, right?

"Okay, we can camp here," I say. "But you have know that it's not legal to camp here. So one thing you have to do. You have to help me turn out the lights when a car comes down the road, okay?"

This proposal arouses some mild awe. Then some serious excitement.

The kids, as always, get it. Bless them. They are our hope.

And this is our camp.

And such is the tone of this dry-land river trip: free form and free spirited.

The next morning, while I sit and read in our illicit campsite in the still-cool early-morning high-desert sun, Webb wakes up. But he doesn't get up: he just lies in his sleeping bag in the van with the door open. Ah, summer mornings! No school this morning? Hell, the World is our school this morning. And on mornings like this, he decides, the best way to attend that school is to stay in bed. So be it.

When the kids do finally get up, we have breakfast, toss everything in the van, then head on down the road (upstream). No itinerary: we just take what we come across on our four-wheeled float. First is the ghost town, where we wander around the old water tank and pumphouse, an old store, a decrepit station. Then we mosey up a little side creek lined with crayfish shells like tossed candy wrappers by snacking birds and raccoons.

Onward. In the afternoon we turn up a dirt two-track up a side stream's valley. The creek is wide with spring melt and its valley a narrow meandering gorge. We drive along the creek, winding with the valley, until we come to a side road down to the creekside. We back down and park. Chairs out. Snacks out. Guitar out. Journals out. We spend the afternoon lolling in the sun like harbor seals, or playing in the swollen-but-shallow stream. For an hour or so I play guitar for the kids, trying to explain the meaning of Neil Young songs ("What's a 'kinder, gentler machine gun hand'?" "Why can't you be twenty on Sugar Mountain?" "Why is it better to burn out than it is to rust?" (so I told them about this guy who's trying to burn as few calories as possible …))

Again, the kids need nothing more than what's here – sticks, rocks, river, grass. Again, I see the rigid rulings of schooling pass out of them like a healthy sweat. Again, though, I feel this myself as the dizziness of daily busyness is flushed from my own system.

And I realize, again, I can't tell my kids the things I'd love to tell them – about how to think, about what school's trying to really teach them, what to do, what's right and wrong, good and bad. I can just bring them to places, let them do stuff, and they'll figure it out for themselves – what ever "it" is for them.

What kids really need is unstructured time in big open spaces. That's pretty much it. Then they'll become whoever they are.

And, really, isn't that the point?

Nighttime on our adventure, and once again we are camped illegally. So while we lie in the van and write and read, the kids gleefully turn out headlamps and the lantern the few times a set of headlights passes up the valley.

And we have a most excellent time.

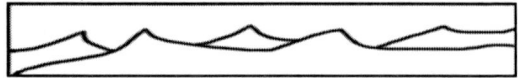

License to Shill

*M*y family and I just got back from Sedona, Arizona, land of lovely pinion-juniper forest, amazing redrock spires and bluffs, glitzy resorts and spiritual energy-field vortexes.

The only vortex we found, though, was the one our credit card number went into.

But we should've known. We headed down from our Colorado home to the self-proclaimed "New Age" capital of the West thanks to a friend, who gave us a free three-day stay at a resort. All we had to do was sit through a short sales pitch for the time-share program our friend was a member of. And for doing that, we would also get a free dinner in town.

This, of course, should have been warning number one. Like my mother always said, If it sounds too good to be true, it probably is.

Still, we treated it like an adventure. We could endure an hour and a half for a dinner and three free nights away in a beautiful place. We were even excited to sit there and check out the sales experience, like the cool skeptics at the hypnotist show.

I didn't know, though, that I'd end up feeling like the guy who passes the show walking around the room on all fours braying like a donkey.

Our show began at 9 a.m. on the second day of our stay. The same day, by the way, that Sedona was hit with the biggest floods in decades, washing cars and RVs down the scenic Oak Creek Canyon, and flowing over the bridge in town. Warning number two. But we missed all that because we were indoors. We hadn't eaten breakfast, because we'd been guaranteed the presentation wouldn't take more than an hour and a half. So while we sat at the little table with Travis, our own personal time-share sales representative, we filled ourselves with a stream of the excellent free coffee.

The scene was every bit the weird, wondrous show we'd expected. Once our group of free-loaders – us and another dozen couples – were all gathered in the lobby, we were herded en masse into a bigger room with expansive windows looking out over a rainy resort courtyard, backed by the area's trademark sandstone monoliths rising impressively in the distance. As we dissolved into the room, each couple was ushered by a sales person to a small round table. Once there, like an orchestrated military movement, the sales pitches commenced at once all around us.

At our table, Travis delivered his own sales pitch. He was a nice guy. Young. Intense. Good looking. Good at what he did. And what he did was, for exactly an hour and a half, make us understand why we, as a family that traveled a fair amount and planned to go abroad several times in the next few years – information we gave freely, because it was true – would be morons and child abusers for not buying into this program, which would get us cheap lodging at sweet resorts all around the world, and that since it's treated as deeded property, we would pay off while using, letting us travel cheaply when we retire, and which our kids would inherit when we finally went on to the great cruise in the sky.

He then brought out a personal photo album of him and his pretty fiancée in beautiful Hawaii on their own recent time-share excursion.

When the hour and half was up, I needed to think about this. Because there was some logic to it – crazy logic, granted – but logic nonetheless. Sarah and I needed to at least talk about it.

"Don't you want to spend quality time with your kids?" he concluded with the sincerity and intensity of a minister.

Yes. I did. Right then, in fact. But our kids were back in the room engorging themselves on snacks with free reign of the TV. Around me, chatter filled the room, dense and energetic, like the caffeine burning an acid hole in my stomach and setting fire to my cerebral cortex.

"You deserve it!"

"A phenomenal lifestyle!"

And, "Buy today … buy today … buy today."

Buy today, Travis continued, urging us, doing us a huge, huge favor, because there were huge incentives and extras being offered right now, and only now, in this room – in fact, if we were to leave this room, the offers would be gone, and the only thing we'd ever again be eligible for is the standard package at the normal retail rate. So, buy today, buy here and buy now.

Corks popped around us as other couples signed on the dotted line and celebrated with little bottles of champagne. I really needed to think about this. So did Sarah. This was a good time to talk, because Travis needed to go see if his regional sales manager, who just happened to be there that day, he said, would let him spice up our offer.

Now, I know you know where this is headed. But let me say, even though we went in to this thing without so much as a dust particle of possibility that we might actually be interested in a time share (actually, there is no "a" for time-share ownership, because even though it's treated like deeded property, what you really "own" are only annually-renewed "points" that can be redeemed for lodging around the world), there was an alluring reasoning unfolding here. Since our kids were now getting older, we've set our sights on doing several big adventures abroad in the next several years, before our kids are on their own. Then we hope to travel ourselves, like we did before we had kids, when our adventuring took us to Europe and Africa. And it would be cool to pass on this incentive to travel to our kids ... It was like an investment in nice lodging around the world for the price of a cheap hotel room, even if we just used the resorts as jumping off points to the more primitive traveling we prefer, and thereby reducing our planning by at least that much ...

A valid train of thought at least worth considering. If we at least had the time and space to consider it.

But we couldn't leave, of course, so instead Travis kept leaving the table so my wife and I could gather our wits and talk. And then he would return just before we could lay the cards out long enough to come to some resolution. And he'd come back with more sweeteners: Two free round-trip airline tickets. A free week of lodging. No fees the first year.

Our kids called our cell phone. How much longer would be?

"Just a few minutes," I whispered gruffly into the phone, feeling the "average to high stress" Travis had scribbled secretly, yet clearly, on the top of the interview form.

"They sound like great kids," Travis cooed, as I pocketed the phone and sat back down.

Then the regional sales manager, a serious, but gentle, older man in a sweater who looked like Andy Griffith in 1963, came by.

Why can't we leave and ponder this? I asked. Pleaded. We wanted desperately to just leave, but this was a big thing, and maybe a big chance, and maybe a really good offer – I mean, our friend does it, right? Lots of people do it, right? Why can't we just leave, soak in the hot tub for an hour, and come back with a decision?

"Because studies have shown," sweater-man answered, "if that happens, our sales go down forty percent."

Warning number three. But, you gotta love the honesty. He then personally authorized an extra several-thousand-dollar discount.

"I am in so much trouble for this," Travis confided with a frown after he left.

Well, you know where this went.

Sounds insane, doesn't it? But we did it. Before we left that room – hours later, and we were the last ones to leave – we had signed away a frightening number of thousands of dollars. And we had put the $1,400 deposit on our credit card.

I brayed like the jackass I was.

Trust me: I take crazy risks, even spontaneous ones, but generally, whenever I can, I pursue those painfully slowly and deliberately. Still, although the caffeine may have been a catalyzing agent, the purchase left us with a rush of excitement, like we'd done something zany that was a long-term investment and, most of all, was going to now force us to live that traveling life we had been envisioning.

Given that, at its best, this time-share arrangement struck me as a brilliant sort of for-profit world-wide commune, a kind of capitalistic socialism for travelers.

At its worst, it was $14,000 worth of advance hotel reservations.

That "worst" part settled in after a couple of hours, after the initial enthusiasm and caffeine wore off, replaced by a margarita and some very late lunch. Then what we had done sank in, like a hari-kari sword.

And that's why they didn't let us step outside and ponder.

After several tense, awkward hours filled with a mildly psychotic blend of giggling and soft whimpering, things turned out fine. We called a lawyer friend who, after he stopped laughing, did some quick internet research and found that Arizona has a seven-day contract rescission law, just for suckers like us. It should even be written into the contract, he added.

We looked again. It was. Right there above our signature.

And right then I understood how old folks get swindled out of their retirement savings. How kids get sucked into crazy cults. How it was that 25 years earlier I had gotten conned out of all my money after being in New York City for only fifteen minutes. How sales-people make their living.

Still, it was all above the board, all legal. And it's hard to blame Travis and his time-share shilling compatriots. We deserved it. We knew what was happening. We signed the contract, willingly, ear-nestly. I felt like a psychology experiment. And as for me and Sarah, it happened to both of us, right before each other's eyes. We couldn't even redeem ourselves by being able to point at the other and bark, You idiot!

In fact, in going back over this experience now, I'll admit that I even feel some admiration for Travis. He was good at what he did – polished, professional, trained, skilled, adaptable. I think even, maybe, somewhere, to some degree, he might have really believed he was doing us a favor, somehow saving our future. I think even we believed it for a few intoxicating hours.

Impressive. But, still, it strikes me as grim work. It was our fault, and it was completely legal, but it was nonetheless deliberately de-ceptive. It was shamelessly manipulative.

Still, Sarah and I learned a lot, about ourselves, and about the great big scary world out there. About how we really want to do our traveling – and which, because of this experience, we're now more than ever determined to do. And we will always hold the Great Time Share Adventure as one of the great stories between us.

Given those positives, maybe this predatory hard-selling has a function in natural selection. Maybe these time-share sales people are like, say, hyenas or dingoes, performing their own Darwinian culling of the dumb, the weak and the confused from the economic herd, and thereby strengthening the survivors.

Maybe. All I know is, I hope my wife and I evolved.

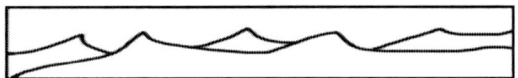

Mexican Hat Vacation

S CENE: *Family seated around dinner table, passing bowls and filling plates (something American: meatloaf, mashed potatoes, green beans kids won't eat, etc.). All are talking at same time. As they start eating, father raises his arms over table. All stop eating and talking to listen.*

FATHER: (Solemnly) Dear Heavenly Goddess ... (Family stares.) Just kidding! Hey I have something exciting to tell you. The magazine is sending me to visit someplace cool this weekend, and we're all going!

MOTHER, SON, DAUGHTER: (Excited chatter.)

DAUGHTER: Where are we going, Dad?

FATHER: (Dramatic pause, then profoundly) Mexican ... Hat ... Utah!

MOTHER, SON, DAUGHTER: (Extended dramatic pause.)

SON: Where we take the boat out when we raft the San Juan?

FATHER: That's right!

DAUGHTER: Is there ... a town there?

FATHER: Well, it's pretty small. And remote. But I feel like the only way we've ever seen Mexican Hat is leaving. I don't think we've ever even driven into town, since our truck's always getting shuttled there. The idea for the article is, no body goes to Mexican Hat to go to Mexican Hat ... so we're going to spend a couple of days there and see what happens!

MOTHER, SON, DAUGHTER: (Extended dramatic pause.)

SCENE: Night. The enormous, gas-guzzling Family Truckster pulls up in dark parking lot. Headlights illuminate an adobe building marked "Trading Post."

SCENE: Father and Mother enter gift shop/inn office. They ring bell. While waiting for service, they study framed black-and-white pictures hanging on wall: first shows a formal-looking group on the metal span of bridge that stands over river just above the Inn. Camera zooms to caption: "Opening of new bridge over San Juan River, 1957." Camera moves to another b&w photograph that shows the cavalry crossing the river toward a great sandstone ridge. The caption here says, "Filming 'She Wore A Yellow Ribbon' below Mexican Hat Rock."

Enter innkeeper.

FATHER: (Politely gives name to stoic innkeeper. Innkeeper begins to flip through pages of enormous notebook.) So, pretty slow this time of year, huh? Now that those ratty river runners have quit for the season. (Laughs and winks at Mother.)

INNKEEPER: (Not looking up, still studying and flipping big pages.) Actually this is our busiest time of year. We start getting busy in July and it lasts until the end of October. Mostly older people and foreigners. One year, it was Japanese, another year Germans. This year it seems to be the French. I can't find you in our reservation book.

FATHER: The magazine I write for was supposed to have reserved and paid for our room.

INNKEEPER: Well, you're not here, but we have one room left. (Mother scowls as father sheepishly pulls out credit card.)

SCENE: Family Truckster pulls into very full parking lot. Looming over the other vehicles, it edges into a row of identical rental cars. The Truckster's doors barely open as family edges out. They cross parking lot and enter their room at the "inn," which, actually, looks just like a motel.

SCENE: Morning. Camera pans to show scene: early morning light illuminates low redrock walls above the thick, grey river ... on the near side of river, the parking lot stands above river and is lined with yellowing autumn cottonwoods. Camera zooms in as family steps out of room and into the parking lot – to find it full of men and women, most dressed in black, walking by in pairs and standing hunched over in small groups, smoking cigarettes and glancing around furtively.

DAUGHTER: Mom, who are these people?

MOTHER: I think these are Europeans, Honey.

DAUGHTER: How do you know, mom?

MOTHER: I lived in France a while.

(A couple dressed in black walks by, gesturing animatedly and mumbling in an indecipherable distant tongue.)

SON: Toto, I don't think we're in Utah anymore …

FATHER: I feel like I'm in that bar-scene in Star Wars …

SCENE: Long-shot: The Family Truckster passes under camera and rolls down highway with the Mexican Hat Rock alongside in the distance. Father's arm points out window at same time Truckster swerves off pavement, kicking up a great cloud of dust, and then squeals back onto roadway and continues on out of sight, leaving only view of great rock spire of Mexican Hat Rock.

SCENE: Inside Family Truckster. Children in backseat jam to Linkin Park playing on Truckster's stereo; Mother knits. Father turns off stereo.

FATHER: Did you know that Emery Langdon Goodridge was the first trader to come to Mexican Hat? (Son and Daughter exchange eye-rolling glances.) He started the trading post where we're staying in 1882. He was looking for gold and oil, but had a good business trading Navajo blankets.

(Silence inside Family Truckster)

MOTHER: That's great, dear.

SON: Put the music back on, Dad.

(Father turns stereo back on, but no sound. CD spits out, and camera zooms to "ERROR" message on stereo. Repeated tries yields same result.)

FATHER: Geez, I guess the CD player's broken. (Groans from back seat.) Well, this is a great chance to get some local flavor on the radio anyway.

(Father fidgets with radio … repeated scans yield country-and-western music on every station, each met with "No!" from the back seat.)

FATHER: Let's try AM, then.

(Father tweaks radio again, but only station found is playing static-laced powwow music. Father leaves it on.)

SCENE: Long shot: To the sounds of powwow music, Family Truckster pulls into a small parking lot at the Goosenecks of the San

Juan State Park overlook. Camera zooms wide to show deep, meandering chasm of the Goosenecks of the San Juan River: The grey river is set a thousand feet below in a great, banded gorge; a long shot shows the canyon to be bent in enormous, beautiful bow-tie turns. In the foreground, several cars – the same rental model found in the inn's parking lot – are parked at the fenced overlook.

SCENE: Series of vignettes set to powwow music: family stands at overlook alongside a dozen gray-haired tourists staring and pointing at the boulder-strewn canyon walls falling down to river a thousand feet below ... family climbs over fence and scrambles down rocks below overlook while tourists back on top gasp and point at family ... back on top, father talks excitedly while pointing to landscape in distance while family looks elsewhere and walks away without his knowing ... mother and daughter try on Native jewelry from old Navajo woman with her wares laid out on blanket at overlook.

SCENE: Family climbs back into Family Truckster.
FATHER: That was neat!
MOTHER, SON, DAUGHTER: Yeah, that was cool, Dad.
FATHER: And now, on to Valley of the Gods!
MOTHER, SON, DAUGHTER: Noooo!
FATHER: No, it's cool. It's a long dirt road across the desert and around some amazing rock spires and towers like a little Monument Valley ...
MOTHER: That's great, dear, but I think we want to just go back and hang out at the Inn. This is a vacation for us. You can go explore if you want, though ...
SON, DAUGHTER: Yeah!
FATHER: Oh, c'mon, guys. It'll be great –
SON, DAUGHTER: Noooo!
FATHER: C'mon – this a family vacation, kids! We can hang around the inn, after that ... I promise.
(Dramatic pause)
DAUGHTER: (Looking resigned) O-kay ...
SON: Can we change the music at least?

SCENE: Series of vignettes set to top-40 country music ...
Family Truckster passes dirt road.
MOTHER (voice over): Isn't that the turn, honey?

Truckster skids to a stop, backs up, and turns down road in a cloud of red dust, camera zooms in on little sign that says "Valley of the Gods" beneath broad escarpment of Cedar Mesa ...
Truckster tailgates enormous RV size of a Greyhound bus with "Wilderness" emblazoned on back, until Truckster is lost in dust cloud ...

Truckster winds in and out of dry washes on road.
FATHER (voice over): Wanna' get out and hike up that ...?
SON, DAUGHTER (voice over): Noooo!
Long shot of Truckster under rust-red rock cliffs.
DAUGHTER (voice over): Hey, Dad. It says in my magazine that the rap singer 50 Cent has been shot nine times!
FATHER (voice over): Well, Sweetie, that's the sign of a slow learner.
Truckster passes over high, rolling hill with long views to the colorful ridgeline of Raplee Anticline in distance.
FATHER (voice over): Kids wouldn't it be great to sleep out here?
SON, DAUGHTER (voice over): Noooo!
Long shot of Truckster grinding away under tall rock spires.
SON (voice over): Dad, can I drive? I've seen "Fast and Furious" like fifty times!"
FATHER (voice over): That's exactly why you're not going to drive. Ask me again when you're 30.
Truckster fades away over desertscape horizon to sounds of country music ...

SCENE: *Inside room at the inn, cramped with two beds, big TV, desk, nightstand.*
SON: C'mon Dad! hang with us! There's nothing going on around here.
MOTHER: Yeah, Honey, let's take a nap ... (She rubs Father's shoulders suggestively.)
FATHER: No. I want to explore! That's why we're here! To see what Mexican Hat has to offer. That's my duty as a reporter!
DAUGHTER: Oh, Dad.
FATHER: Besides, you know how easily I get cabin fever ... (Dramatic pause.)
MOTHER: You're right, honey. (Son and Daughter nod in agreement.) We'll see you later.

SCENE: Father steps out onto sidewalk. Nearby, a group of four people dressed in black are hunched over, scowling, smoking cigarettes. They peer at Father as he walks away ... Camera follows Father, zooming wider, as Father looks determined, walking along, looking around ... he walks past camera, up hill out of inn parking lot – a sandstone wall lines left side of driveway and highway. The camera watches as he crosses the highway and struts up the right side of the highway. Off to his right, past a guardrail, the embankment falls away quickly to the swift river. Camera comes into focus on distant signs of town – the tin shed of the Mexican Hat Volunteer Fire Department ... a lonely motel ... an adobe tipi ... a sterile modern gas station ... a double-wide trailer ... Sounds: several dogs bark eagerly, almost savagely ...

As Father marches over the hill and out of sight, the camera focuses and settles on the distant bluffs ... and the Mexican Hat Rock looming, in its tiny, distant way, above town.

SCENE: Long shot: In front of the inn, on the ledge between the parking lot and river, are several grassy spots beyond which a cliff falls thirty feet to the river. There are a few picnic tables, and some metal lawn furniture, in which recline Mother, Daughter, and Son.

Camera zooms in. Father, dust covered to the point of being pale, walks up to family.

MOTHER: How was it?

FATHER: Well, I think it will be good preparation for visiting the Australian outback.

(Father drops tiredly on to empty lounge chair next to family, sighing heavily.)

SON: So, Dad, what's your story going to say?

FATHER: Son, I'm not sure there's a story here after all ...

Meanwhile as family, all reclining in their lounge chairs, stare at Father ... camera zooms back and away ... above inn, where dozens of people, smoking and dressed in black, pace up and down the parking lot ... camera continues higher, above lovely redrock ridges lining river ... above metal-arch bridge spanning San Juan River.

FATHER (voice over): But on my walk I did come up with another place to visit, where I think it would be cool for us to go next time to see what it's like ...

Camera continues to rise ... above Mexican Hat's half-mile long strip of motels and stores and its single modern convenience store/gas station complex ... higher, until above it all Mexican Hat Rock looms in distance backdropped by the dramatic and colorful chevron-shaped outcroppings of the Raplee Anticline ...off to the right appear the grand spires of Monument Valley ... to the left comes into view the great Goosenecks of the San Juan as the little town becomes a speck on the landscape ...

FATHER (voice over): ... next time, Hanksville!

Fade to black.

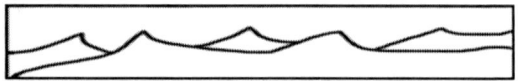

The Place Too Few Knew

I'm walking across a broad, meadowed valley. One side of the valley is a high, steep ridgeline, furry with scrub oak, and frosted with pinion and juniper and ponderosa. The other side is a long, low forested mountain that at night is dotted with blinking red bulbs. To the east, a rocky, blocky mountain stands guard over the narrow notch that is the outlet canyon for the valley's creek; and to the west is the inlet, where the valley slopes gently toward a low divide.

It's quiet except for the melodic whistles of meadowlarks and redwing blackbirds. Soon those will be replaced, after the sun finishes its sunset finale, by the chattering of spring frogs and the yipping of coyotes.

This is how it used to be all around here, in southwestern Colorado, particularly around this middle-portion of the Animas River, amidst the foothills of the La Plata Mountains where hard-edged ridges roll off into the high desert like a frozen line of surf. This area used to be loaded with undeveloped and little-visited valleys and ridges and basins. Now, though, how much of this area is getting brought into the real-estate fold? Much of it. Most of it. Nearly all.

Yet this big wild remnant valley is just five minutes from downtown Durango. How blessed is that? So blessed it ought to be protected. And, actually, it was. But it's not any more. And it won't be the wild place it has been for so long much longer, either.

Ridges Basin is still how it used to be around here, a living little piece of the big outside – open, wild, accessible, healthy country – yet close to town. And protected as public land, too – there for the people and the wildlife, forever.

Well, that's how it was supposed to be, anyway. And it is still that way, for now. But it's going fast. Already, bulldozers scrape away fertile earth that was laid down by the glaciers, dynamite blasts rock that was exposed when the La Platas formed, and soon water will fill an area that has supported people and wildlife for thousands of years. Now Ridges Basin hums with not just birdsong, elk bugles, and coyote howls, but with diesel engines and traffic and explosions. And if all goes as planned and the government funding keeps pouring in, soon the penstocks will close on Ridges Basin Dam, and Ridges Basin Reservoir will begin to submerge rare and vital wildlife habitat, historical artifacts, and archaeological sites.

And for those of us who love and need big, undeveloped landscapes as part of their regular diet, ALP it will also drown another chunk of out there right here.

So, I try to savor Ridges Basin while it's still here. I know it's a hospice service – a heart-wrenching caring for a dying friend – but I need to see it, taste it, be with it while I can. Like I do today.

On this lovely early-spring day, I parked on the side of County Road 211, the dirt track that runs the length of the basin. From here, I headed out on foot southward, across the big plain, away from the road toward Basin Ridge, the southern flank of the valley. Spring-green grass and weed shoots carpet the ground, speckled with a few colorful early wildflowers. Mixed in for good measure are elk droppings, hair-filled coyote scat, prairie dogs and their holes (and their predators: a few months ago, I found a fresh gut-shot badger, target practice for some Friday-afternoon gun slinger). And if I sat and looked long enough, I'd probably see one of the three pairs of bald eagles that nest here, or the Peregrine falcon known to frequent the basin.

How does all this wildlife manage to live here, just five minutes from greater metro Durango? From the middle of the valley I can see how: the surrounding forested foothills … the tops of the snowy La Platas poking over the ridge … the absolute quiet in all directions. Ridges Basin provides a sanctuary right in the midst of the roads and houses and golf courses that the Animas Valley has become, while offering an essential migration corridor linking the wild country in the La Patas with the pinion-juniper badlands to the south.

And now, with the coming of more of that growth gobbling up what little winter range and migration routes are left in the valley, Ridges Basin, just as it's being butchered, is more needed than ever.

I soon hit Basin Creek. This is another reason so many animals find sanctuary here: year-round water in a semi-arid land. Ridges Basin is a unique water catch: a clay layer under the topsoil holds water, creating wetlands and keeping the ground damp and fertile even in dry times. The creek itself is set in a shallow draw, lined with reeds and rushes and cattails and cottonwoods and home to birds and insects and crayfish (the bank is littered with their hollow claws, dropped by feeding birds and animals like candy wrappers).

People, too have found a home here. Most recently, the Bodo family worked this land since 1914. Their homestead and ranching remnants still can be found throughout the basin. On this walk, as I mosey westward, up the creek, I eventually come upon a Cadillac Ranch-sort of display – the hulks of a dozen old cars emerge from the ground where someone had tried to reinforce the stream bank decades earlier. Off to the left hides an old outhouse, alone and abandoned off in the trees (with a great view, of course). Just upstream of the cars, set in a deep cut next to a low foothill, stands a breached old dam that once fed a series of hand-dug irrigation ditches.

The Bodo family gave up ranching in the 1970s, but not their love of the land that fed their family for generations. In 1974, they sold their land to the Nature Conservancy, with a heart-felt wish written as a clause in the deed: that Ridges Basin stay wild for wildlife forever. And when the Nature Conservancy turned over the basin to the Colorado Division of Wildlife, becoming the Bodo Wildlife Area, that clause remained intact. Today, an estimated 300 mule deer reside here, and as many as 1,000 migrate through in the fall; 100 elk live here year-round, and another 400 winter here; and in May and June, the basin serves as vital elk calving grounds.

A wild place for wild life, and public land for the Durango area's wild people. Forever.

Forever, that is, until the Bureau of Reclamation decided it needed the basin for the Animas-La Plata Project, perhaps the government's last great Western water project, the last gasp of the era of big dams.

In 1991, when the CDOW had to deny access to BuRec to do some testing for ALP, BuRec simply condemned 4,000 acres of the Bodo Wildlife Area – the hell with the "public" in public land, or the "wildlife" in Wildlife Area, or the "forever" clause the CDOW was entrusted with. Ridges Basin's death sentence was issued.

And for what is Ridges Basin being sacrificed? Let's have a quick review. Now, I admit this review is blatantly biased, but let's be blunt here: ALP is greedy and stupid, and there's no way anyone with a heart bigger than a silver dollar or warmer than a pocket calculator can justify it – unless they'll be profiting from it.

ALP will cost taxpayers a quarter to a third of a billion dollars so it can pump water uphill, store it, then let it run back down to the Animas River a couple of miles downstream of where it was first extracted. And what's that water to be used for? Yes, public water supply is part of it (even though that "need" was based on the inflated national water-use average of 179 gallons per person per day). It was the satisfaction of Indian water claims that finally sold ALP, though, after the project had stalled on its own indefensible financial and ecological arguments.

And what will this "Indian" water be used for? Here's the primary shopping list:

- 2,400 acre-feet per year (an acre-foot is roughly the amount of water consumed by a thirsty family of four in a year) for several golf courses around the region, including one here on the shores of Ridges Basin Reservoir.
- 17 af/yr for three new resorts and a dude ranch in the same places
- 4,600 af/yr for a new gas-fired power plant
- 830 af/yr for a new coal mine
- and 27,000 af/yr for a new coal-fired power plant – which, of course, will help supply the as much as 160 million kilowatt-hours of electricity required each year to pump Animas River water 500 feet uphill to Ridges Basin.

Evaporation loss alone is estimated to suck away 2,235 acre-feet from the surface of the reservoir each year.

Stupid. Wasteful. Greedy.

m

The Bodo family may have retired from ranching, but Ridges Basin hasn't stopped feeding people.

One night recently I wandered the empty county road in the near-full moonlight. As I approached one of the turnouts off the road, I could see a square light from a dimly-lit trailer. Then something else caught my eye: some kind of big, bright mass in the meadow behind the trailer moving gently in unison, like a slow, luminous eddy. As I got close enough for the moonlight to be enough light, the scene came together: An old, rounded sheepherder's wagon stood in the turnout, and behind it a flock of sheep (600 head, I would soon learn) grazed and dozed in the basin.

As I stood there in awe, in appreciation, relishing the unexpected spectacle, out of the trailer came the sheepherder himself.

We talked while he shined his big flashlight over his charges. "The want to move in the moonlight," he said. "I probably won't sleep much tonight."

He introduced himself as just "Nelson," "a Navajo Indian from Cuba," he told me. "Do you know where Cuba is?" he asked.

"New Mexico?" I answered.

"Right," he admitted, seeming a little bummed that I didn't fall for his ploy by mistaking it for the Caribbean Cuba.

Nelson was driving the flock to Ignacio, some 25 miles away, for lambing, having walked from New Mexico, a few days earlier. He would cross the basin tomorrow, pushing the sheep down to the Animas, and on into Ignacio a few days later. After lambing, he would then walk them up into the high country for the summer.

It amazed me that this still went on – that people still had jobs that meant they walked for a week. That's my kind of job, I was thinking … thinking maybe I'm not too old for a job change.

Not too old, but too late: Nelson informed me that, after 100 years, this was this outfit's the last sheep drive ever through Ridges Basin. Why? Because next year the dam site will be impassable.

"They're going to have to find a new way across the Ute reservation," he told me. "It will be hard on the animals."

Then we were silent for a while. The moon beamed on, urging the sheep on down the valley, toward the river.

Nelson turned on his big beam and flashed it again over the restless flock.

"Why do they have to ruin good country?" he asked, breaking the silence.

I didn't have an answer for him this time.

Nelson's outfit, nor the Bodo family, were the first. There's a long history of people living and making a living in Ridges Basin.

As I walk on, I move up the little hill next to the dam site. On the top of the hill I'm surprised to find a series of excavated holes. I wonder what I've stumbled upon, until I see bits of painted clay potsherds scattered across the ground. Then I realize I've found a set of ancient pit houses and the round depression marking the site of a prehistoric kiva.

Ridges Basin was visited and utilized as far back as 13,000 years ago by roving hunters and gatherers, but the first verified habitation is 8,000 years ago. Some 30 sites of these migratory "archaic" Indians have been identified in Ridges Basin. But they were just the beginning of thousands of years of use and habitation. Those first basin residents were then followed by the corn-growing and foraging "Basketmaker II" Indians and their pit-house dwellings; they then gave way to the so-called Early Puebloans, who had above-ground masonry in the pueblos, storage units, and kivas. More than a hundred of their sites have been identified in Ridges Basin.

Sites like I've found today lie hidden all over the basin, and they are an irreplaceable prehistoric record. They also are a testament to the health and vitality of this place as a home and resource for people as well as wildlife. But it's a record you have to come out and read now, or not at all: An estimated 1,300 to 1,400 of these archeological sites will be flooded by Ridges Basin reservoir or damaged in the building and rerouting of three pipelines, a powerline, and C.R. 211.

Why do they have to ruin good country? Erase 8,000 years of history? Ravage yet another in a dwindling stash of undeveloped country – for both the wildlife we all love and those of us who love wildlife and wild country?

I still have no answer for Nelson, or myself, or my kids who have grown to love this place.

The sun is setting on Ridges Basin – both metaphorically, and physically for me on my walk. The western sky is a thick band of pastels giving way to some pinpoint stars overhead. Alpenglow slides up the face of Carbon Mountain as the big bright ball of the moon stands above, sliding up the darkening sky. As I walk across the basin back toward my truck in moonlight and starlight, the spring frogs start chattering, and the first coyote yips announce dinner time for all. I aim toward the red-eyed radio tower lights blinking on Smelter Mountain – the same lights I can see from the front porch of my house.

Have you ever looked at some familiar ridge near your own home wondered what's on the other side?

You should. You should find out, while you still can. If you can stand to really see what's being lost.

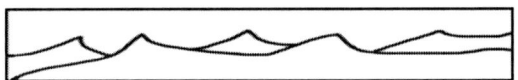

Let Us Now Praise Weeds!

*A*typically lovely Four Corners morning – diamond-clear and as brilliant as a bright idea. So while the air's still cool I decide to mow the lawn. Such as it is, in our case. Typical Four Corners, again: aside from my wife's colorful gardens, our yard is generally dry, spotty, downright dusty in places, with islands of what is recognizable as "lawn" growth dotted with puddles of richer, healthier weed gene pools.

Today the dandelions are doing particularly well, expanding their collective reach into the thirsty grass like a rising sea level. I mow them down, as is my urban duty, shredding their serrated leaves and decapitating their complex little buttery-yellow heads. But I don't feel bad – I know they ain't dead. They're weeds – resilient and adaptable and clever. And I know my intent is not to kill. I look at it as more like ... caching. I keep my secret crop on the lowdown for some hard time when it'll be needed to flourish, because every part of the everyday dandelion is edible, and can be used for everything from nutritional greens to a coffee substitute to wine.

I've always had some kind of weak spot for weeds. When my wife and I lived in Boulder, I tried to keep our half of our duplex's lawn as feral as possible. It was an interesting experiment, I thought, to see what exactly would happen to a piece of ground left to the sculpting of the region's natural semi-arid climate. The grass, obviously not from around these parts, quickly faltered, paled, and perished. But not long after, a succession of new and fascinating vegetative homesteaders arrived, took root, and happily, healthily flourished in their newfound outpost of high prairie.

They were weeds, to be sure ... but that's what weeds do – they find fulfillment in what's available, what's there, what's offered, in things as they are. I like that in an organism of any kind. Not everyone feels that way, though, and one day there was a nasty-looking piece of official paper on our door with the crest of the People's Republic of Boulder on it, demanding that I cease and desist my ... well, my ceasing and desisting at watering and mowing and pruning the piece of land that people can see from the public sidewalk.

I found someone who understood my peculiar pro-weed sympathies when we moved to downtown Durango. Our neighbor was a friendly middle-aged bachelor, who, in the fashion of males left unguided, took minimal care of his lawn. Good care – no doubt, and way beyond my own personal proclivities – but being a professional ecologist, he appreciated and endeavored to work his social obligations within the realities of the Four Corners' climate.

Except on the northeast side of his house, in a cool, shady dead zone between his bathroom wall and our fence. There, in a three-foot-by-six-foot parcel, he and I conspired to offer a small piece of ground to wildness, and see what happened.

What happened was, while we each titrated just enough water on our yards to keep our immigrant grasses alive – bordering on some kind of plant water torture, I'm sure – our feral little parkland freaked out with a stunning diversity of plant life. First the usual: dandelions and bindweed and such – but, later, in the dry hot days of August, spurred with some afternoon thunderstorms, culminating in a tall, dense stand of swaying green grasses between our residences.

It was beautiful. And mostly native grasses, my neighbor observed, rattling off the Latin names of each plant with some awe over how quickly and deftly they had returned. Thanks, of course, to the pioneering preparation of that front line of weeds.

But a neighbor like that is a rarity when you live downtown, and everyone has to look at your strange affection evolve alongside the sidewalk. The other day, for example, I was over talking to another neighbor, whose yard is a magnificent botanical spectacle as lush as a Belgian garden. My neighbor was all decked out in leather gloves, big straw hat, and gardening khakis, and was diligently pulling up long strands of bindweed that had snaked their sneaky way into the golf-course quality grass.

Watching, I couldn't help but comment, with all sincerity and sensitivity, that I rather liked bindweed. They're really a string of lovely little morning glories, I waxed poetically, trying to impress her with my knowledge of local weed lore .... just tiny versions of the regal Evening primrose that blesses the hillsides naturally around here ...

I knew it was true, because I harbored a partial pasture of pink-and-white bindweed blossoms in my own backyard. But I never got to telling her about that, because our conversation was over right about then, as my neighbor quietly refocused on her task at hand, purifying the ground of those tenacious weeds.

I just wandered back to across the street to the feral diversity of my own yard. To my own habitat. To my own weedy kind.

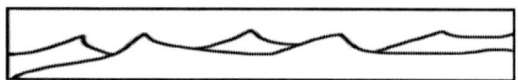

Confessions of an Eco-Trekkie

Eyes front. The unknown is that way.
Captain Kathryn Janeway

*I*t's Thursday night at our house, and that means TV. Dinner over and kitchen cleaned. Homework done. Chores accomplished. So Sarah and I and the kids gather together on the big couch in front of the small screen and take our weekly voyage – meaning Voyager, as in *Star Trek: Voyager*.

Voyager was the third of four shows to spin off of the original *Star Trek* television series, which first aired more than 40 years ago. The Voyager series ran from 1995 to 2001, and depicted the adventures of the starship Voyager, which, while on a mission to capture a band of rebels, is hurled to "the Delta Quadrant" – the most distant and unknown corner of the galaxy. Finding themselves in unexplored space 75 years from Earth even at maximum speed (which is pretty fast in the 24th Century), Voyager's crew and the surviving rebels must work together to get Voyager back across the galaxy to home.

The story of the far-flung crew is vintage Star Trek: high-tech, whiz-bang science fiction adventure. Also like the original series, though, Voyager offers in that sci-fi framework timeless, Homeric, heroic tales (free of the modern need for sarcastic cynicism and gratuitous sex and violence). They may take place in space, but these are stories of people just like us: seeking understanding amidst diversity, character amidst challenge, meaning amidst vastness, and humanity amidst technology. Journeys into humanness.

We are addicts.

This revelation may startle some people. To be honest, I don't talk about it much, because among my closest associates I'm known as an anti-technology Luddite, the bare-footed primitivist, some kind of tree-hugging dirt worshipper.

Well, my friends, consider me outed. Add to that list: shameless Trekkie.

Plus, I admit that I am now deliberately, methodically, and reverently passing that condition onto my kids.

To explain this, I need to make another confession: That it's not technology I rebel against. I resist what technology is used for – to abuse the land, to enrich the few, to suppress points of view and oppress people. And on the individual level, I revolt against using technology the way so many people do today: as a replacement for thinking, for seeing, for skill, for a sense of presence in physical space, for self-entertainment, for social interaction, for cultural understanding, for political involvement, for self-image, for, generally, really experiencing what is out there, in the world around us, whether that's the neighborhood, the nearby countryside, or the other side of the galaxy.

My philosophy is: You yourself are responsible for your journey.

And that, right there, is the message of Star Trek: that if we can get a handle on that principle as individuals first, then as a culture and society (or, to better reflect the diversity celebrated in Star Trek, if we can do that as many individuals, all cultures, and varied societies) then technology can be used to better and deepen our journeys as human beings exploring the mystery of life in a grand and unfathomable universe.

We can be explorers, rather than exploiters, if we choose to make it so.

Quite a vision. And it's a perspective I want my kids to hear and ponder. Because, as far as I can see, the view of the future proffered on Star Trek is the only positive story of where we're headed offered anywhere right now.

Think: What shared stories of our future are available today? Here's a quick list, just off the top of my head: Apocalypse (climate change, disease, famine, etc.). Armageddon (war, Judgment Day, nuclear holocaust, and so on). Extinction (meteor strike, biological meltdown, or somesuch). Or, the shiniest long-term guiding vision on the market today: that we'll somehow muddle through the chaos and climate change and population growth and intermittent warfare if we just keep on keeping on, making it up as we go, trusting in the free market and our government leaders and corporate CEOs …

Can you find the common denominator in the above lineup? Take your pick: Helplessness. Lack of guiding principle. Visionary void. Personal powerlessness. General bleakness. Absence of any sense of what to do, how to do it, or – most importantly – *why* to do it.

This is no way to live. Or to raise kids.

Star Trek, though, offers an option: a path toward a long-term vision, via individual action.

Engage. And embrace.

Engage with your world – because that's why we're here, and nothing can engage it for you. And embrace that world and the others in it, because we're all on this journey in this place – or this space – together.

Bridging that chasm between individual responsibility and a responsible society, Star Trek's model of the United Federation of Planets is a sort of civilized tribalism, or tribal civilization, built on embracing an unlimited array of individuals and cultures ("infinite diversity in infinite combinations," it's called in the show) who work together to more richly engage the universe with the help of technology that is liberating rather than enslaving, creative rather than destructive.

It's as good a vision as any – and better than any I know of – of what we can struggle toward, and of why we should struggle onward.

That's why, at our house, we engage Star Trek every Thursday.

Just so my eco-friends and cohorts know, I haven't sold out my Luddite ideals. I consider these Thursday gatherings as unmediating the media: We use Star Trek as our communal campfire time when my family comes together to share stories that become prompts for pondering and conversation – even if the source of both the "campfire" and stories we share is the technology of television.

Even if it's usually abused – for popular manipulation and personal sedation – it's impossible to deny the effectiveness of television. And I would argue that the television series is the most powerful text every created: it combines the visual, visceral absorption power of film with the deep, empathetic unfolding and evolution of events and characters over a multi-year pattern, like life. And thanks to another technological evolution – by-mail DVD rentals – we are now able to control that text, to cut out the commercial and insert the ritual of exploring Voyager's seven seasons, together.

So every Thursday night at our house, we eat, get our work done, and come together, like families have done for millions of years, but in our modern-world fashion, to embrace our time together, and to engage in stories, and ideas, and visions of where we're all headed. Like people always have. Like, I hope – no, like I am working for – that people will always do.

Meanwhile, on the screen, Captain Kathryn Janeway of the Starship Voyager is making first contact with a new alien species. "We're Humans," she offers by way of introduction, followed by the summary of what that means in one succinct guiding sentence: "We're explorers."

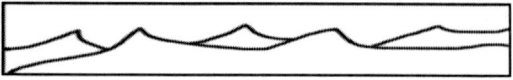

Car Trek

W e were boldly going where no one had gone before ...
Well, in a way no one – or none of us, anyway – has gone
before.

Where we were going was north. Our two-month mission: To
explore the spine of our beloved Rocky Mountains, as far as we could
get (and back) over the summer.

How we were going, though, was the real adventure: In an RV.
Specifically, in a 24-foot camper trailer to be pulled by our trusty
Chevy steed and its stable of 350 horses.

RVs ... I know. I curse them, too. Living in a mountain town that
panders to tourists, vacationers, and silver-haired, white-knuckled
retirees driving Greyhound buses converted to homes nicer than I
was raised in, I, too, have suffered. I have been damned, dammed behind these tin-can condos as they've labored up Coal Bank and Lizard Head passes like mastodons running a marathon. I've watched
with a perverse mix of dread and lurid anticipation as they've wob-
bled unsurely down US 550's sheer switchbacks across the San Juans
like poodles trying to run with the wolves. And I've displayed stunning restraint dodging their weaving ways as they've negotiated our
city's down-town streets and intersections, stopping, starting, and
turning awkwardly like whales schooling with mackerel.

The source of my arrogance is that my wife and I have long been
outdoor purists: backpackers, car campers, river runners, and commercial guides. In all those decades, we've always slept – and, for
several summers, lived – under either canvas or the stars, and the
biggest "motor coach" we've employed has been a 1981 Jeep Wagoneer. And we have endeavored to raise our two children the same
proudly primitive way.

Yet here we be. We be RV.

We therefore knew going into it that this summer would be about more than adventure and travel; it would also involve a cultural leap as new members of RV nation. So we went into it with the only attitude we could: we wouldn't just explore strange new worlds, we would also seek out new life, and a new civilization.

Nonetheless, there is some history here. When she was a kid, my wife's family spent many summers touring the West with the aid of a pop-up tent camper. (Think: two parents and five kids in a little nylon box. Even we're not that tough.) My parents, meanwhile, sported a pickup camper for our family's many New England forays on weekends and vacations. For four of us it was crammed – the kitchen had to be dismantled into a bed every night – but it worked.

Although we both later swore off camper-aided camping, these family RV epics are treasured memories for Sarah and me. So when we decided to make some epic memories with our kids, an RV, for the first time, started to make sense. It would be four of us out on the road for eight weeks, covering a lot of miles and moving our camp a lot. And we would be frequently and for long periods of time in grizzly habitat, so the hard shell around us was comforting. Given those parameters, what we ended up with was a used 24-foot Fleetwood Mallard camper trailer. (The name is important here: Something inside me – perhaps that manly part of me that refuses to wear Lycra or walk around in clogs – wouldn't let me drive an enormous vehicle called what some RVs are named: Swinger. Wilderness. Cherokee. Zeppelin. Chateau Sport. Frolic. Slumber Queen. To name a few.)

Inside the Mallard's thin tin walls are the usual RV amenities: gas stove, small refrigerator, kitchen area, battery (or plug-in AC) power, water, and a good amount of storage space. Getting one of such length also offered us a toilet with a separate wash area, a "master" double bed, a couch that converts to a bed, and another fold-out berth-style bunk. These sleeping options made it so we didn't need to break down the kitchen table to sleep all four of us, so I could keep up my habit of getting up early and brewing coffee and scribbling. It's tight, but it also provided enough space so that over two months we didn't end up living out some RV version of *The Shining*.

It worked. With the help of our RV, we spent this summer exploring our home mountains – visiting our national parks and honoring our public lands (before the Bush administration turns them into Six Flags Over Yellowstone, McGlacier, and Disneycanyonlands), and we got to do it in a way that was fun and functional. Not that we couldn't have done it otherwise, but covering that much ground in such varied terrain and through all kinds of weather was made much easier, secure, and comfortable.

Over two months and thousands of miles, we were always able to pull up to a spot – a campsite, a side road, a pull out in the woods or along a river or on a grand overlook with a sweeping view of the Rockies – and immediately be there. Rain or shine, cold or hot, all we had to do was park, balance the "foundation" with four jacks, turn on the hot water and water pump, and we were home. (Or more like "at the cabin," anyway. Same cabin, new cabin site each night.) And then, if we wanted, it took just five minutes to unhook the truck, and we were off exploring deeper into our new terrain. And on those rainy nights – or when the mosquitoes were thick as rain – we gathered inside, dry and chipper, playing cards or reading.

Comfortable, but this has also been a deeply humbling experience. Actually driving an RV, and not just pointing and cursing, has imparted in me a surprisingly elevated stature for my fellow RV jockeys. As we all know, you don't have to be an astronaut to pilot an RV – but it ain't for sissies, either. Even as a commercial river guide, I have to admit that for generation of sheer fear, whitewater has nothing on hauling a small house on wheels over a mountain road. Think of hours and hours of non-stop class III – no pool-drop rush-relax cycles on the highway – interspersed with frequent, unpredictable class IV pitches: hills, narrow roads, potholes, etc. Even walking through grizzly country is less dangerous than sharing a winding and narrow Northcountry road with tandem tanker semis and ancient overloaded logging trucks careening toward you – and who, like sharks in a swimming pool, know they'll win any confrontation.

In the spirit of full disclosure, I also have to admit that while driving this beast through city streets for needed resupply stops, I came to understand for the first time the value of The Box Store That Must Not Be Named – let's call it Valdemart – for the RVer. It's with great relief that an RV captain spies that huge pavement harbor for throwing out anchor, knowing that this is the one port required to gather the provisions needed to set sail again.

Still, even if I have come to appreciate and empathize with my RVing brothers and sisters, there are some places that, after sharing campgrounds with all sorts of RVs and RVers, my Thoreauvian conscience (and, lest we forget, Thoreau passed his Walden wilderness adventure in a cabin about the size of our RV) won't let me go:

- I will never camp in a Valdemart parking lot.
- No generators. There's nothing more suburban than the camper that pulls into the campground slot next to you, then fires up a whiny engine so the occupants can sit inside by themselves all night watching TV.
- Also for us, no TV. Some campgrounds have cable-TV hookups, and some RVs even have their own satellite dishes that rise from the roof like Eyewitness News vans covering a prison riot. But even in a campground, we're still there to see the land and meet the people.
- No road hogging. When I drive, I always pull over when there's more than three vehicles stacked up behind us. It's a way of "paying it forward" for when I return to my RV-following life back home.
- And we refuse to get one of those spare-tire covers for the back of our camper that says "Easy does it!" or "We're the Wrights! from Durango, Colorado!" Ours instead says "Hayduke Lives!" Hey, I haven't changed that much.

Aside from those who indulged in those nasty behaviors, I have to say, I really liked most of the fellow RVers we met on the road and in campgrounds up and down the great Rocky Mountains. The retired couple (okay, it appears everybody driving around in an RV is retired) who carried their Harley in the back of their RV, using their camper as a base camp. Greg and Katy, hot springs addicts from Vancouver, who, after giving us guidance on springs and spas all over the region, left us with these solemn, sincere parting words of RV wisdom: Don't hit a moose. Bob, Mirna, Roger, and Sue, who shared many beers and many rounds of their home-made beanbag-toss game. The guy who helped build the Alaska Highway who knocked on our door to talk for an hour about how I handle pulling a trailer with an automatic transmission on mountain passes (I shift it like a manual), then left us with maps and his insider insights on camping and fishing spots.

While these are not people we would normally run into camping the way we usually camp, they were still fun. They were friendly. They were interesting. They were … well, travelers, just like us. And I think we found with these folks a deeper connection here than I, in my mountain-man machismo, was ever willing to admit before.

Look, even though I'm now officially an RVer, I still don't think RVing as worthy of the term "camping." No, this is more like … cabining. But if you think about it, the RV and its lifestyle comes from a longer lineage than perhaps we backcountry snobs care to admit. While Europeans tend to idealize exploration in unexplored terra incognita in small (and generally male) parties, the fact is, the way primal people for millions of years really did most of their traveling and migrating was in family groups – and in groups of families – carrying their complete homes along known trails to re-visited and shared camping areas, which minimized impacts, offered security, and guaranteed amenities.

I would like to posit, then, that perhaps the RV is a modern-day technological version of that ancient form of travel, reflecting the nature of the "trail" system we have today. Today's RVs run like wagons or travois or carts or pack animals across the landscape – their occupants something like Bedouins, or gypsies, or the American prairie horse cultures. And RVers then rendezvous nightly in campgrounds or on back roads, remote byways, and roadside turnouts, gathering in tight little self-protecting circles, sharing company and amenities and stories.

Perhaps the RV, seen in this new light, is just the evolutionary step between the tipi and the starship. I mean, isn't that exactly where were are as a culture? Aren't we all just a little RV?

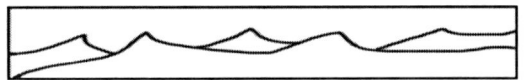

You Can Go Home Again (and Again)

*I*t was a gem of an opportunity – to make the 100-or-so-mile loop around the White Rim, in Canyonlands National Park. But the plan was for Sarah and some friends to ride their mountain bikes while I followed in our little truck, hauling the camping gear and our kids. We brought Webb's and Anna's bikes, but I was expecting three days in the truck with the kids listening to their iPod mixes of angst-filled teen-rebel anthems. I figured I'd be the one whimpering, "Are we there yet?"

Still, I was looking forward to getting back to Canyonlands. See, my life changed there once, and I believe this place midwifed that rebirth, and molded who I've been since. Yes, I'm one of "those" people: Where I am is Who I am.

And, damn, I love who I am here, even if I am just a lowly "sag wagon" driver. Where I am is at the top of the Shafer Trail, looking out over the great gaping gorgeous gorge of the Colorado River, and past, to the distant ragged wall of the already-fall-brown Sierra La Sal. And I'm watching my wife and kids and our friends roll off on their bikes down the big, insanely steep switchbacks toward the White Rim, a scrub-covered white-edged bench stretched out above the river, a couple thousand feet below us.

This is, I believe, cause for ceremony. Because I'm one of those people. And because I'm glad I'm not driving the other sag wagon, an enormous white diesel pickup with a camper on its back. More of a shag wagon, really, I'm thinking as I climb into my nimble little truck and open a beer and plug in a CD. "Only a rat can win a rat race," explains Michael Franti, with a beat. It's been a long time since I was that kind of rat …

To make a short story long, in the early 1980's I spent my first of several winters ski bumming in Colorado – telemarking all day and driving a bus at night. This was supposed to be temporary; I intended to go back to Boston, where I had family, friends, a good-paying job, a serious girlfriend, a brand new sofa, etc. (Yes, I used to be one of those people.) But when the end of the ski season came, I was still there. Something from beyond my good sense and reason was speaking, and it was saying: Where you are is who you are ...

That mysterious voice sounded a lot like my new-found Colorado girlfriend, actually. She was a wild young aspiring writer who could be highly persuasive on matters of adding oddity and adventure to one's lifestyle. She was definitely one of those people. We would, over the next few years, have a great many far-flung adventures together, before she would one day find she could not resist the adventure of running off with our favorite local bartender (margaritas were her weakness). Before those adventures and that heartbreak, though, we would spend one glorious spring on our own sort of Western walk-about – passing a month living out of the back of her car in the Island in the Sky district of Canyonlands National Park.

And it was here my new self was carved – the Colorado Plateau Bum I would henceforth proudly and unbendingly aspire to. I wanted to be one of those people.

At the bottom of the switchbacks, the Shafer Trail meets the White Rim Trail, a 60-mile-plus winding dirt-and-rock track that meanders along the rimrock bench, above the Colorado River and below the Island in the Sky mesa. I stop, and Sarah and the kids roll up. I'm quite impressed Webb and Anna rode their mini-mountain bikes all the way down that hair-ball descent, and tell them so. They are obviously proud themselves, and also appear surprised how much they're enjoying the riding. They'd like to ride more, they say, which is fine with me. I figure they'll tucker out soon enough.

I follow behind the kids, who follow Sarah and the others and imitate them by standing on their pedals and body-englishing the rock riffles, then jamming down sand flats. In places I can look down some of the sidecanyons and see the green, tamarisk-wrapped ribbon of the Colorado River. Well, that deserves a celebration, too; so I crack another beer. My arm hangs out the window, the sun screams into the sunroof (although to the east, the La Sals are sporting some serious meteorological headwear), and REM sings ("What's the frequency, Kenneth?").

The kids pound on.

The Colorado river spurs more memories ... my wife and I first dated while we guided river trips on the Colorado, although upstream a good ways from here. The river molded our relationship, so, like the river, as we grew closer we kept moving downstream, toward the canyons ... in boats, in cars, in love with each other and the landscape and the life here. And finding out that we liked who we were here.

Our first night on the rim finds us camped on the sage flats above the exposed White Rim rock. The La Sals are gone, lost in the general blue-grey cloudmass that has coalesced. Overhead, coming over the mesa top, is the steely bottom of a thunderhead. We cook dinner to the super-slow beat of distant thunder, then gather in a folding-chair circle to watch the approaching lightning, and relax. Everyone is tired – 20-plus miles today. (I know for myself, my right foot and arm are exhausted.) Webb and Anna pedaled more than 15 of those 20 miles, and Sarah and I babble on to our bemused friends about how cool that is. The kids, meanwhile, continue to bomb around the rimrock on their bikes.

The next day is clear, but the moisture that was clouding the sky the night before has fallen onto the road as a heavy overnight rain. I warn the kids that it could be tough biking, so they can ride with me if they want. They look at me with that look. So off go the bikers, and I rumble on behind. Arrested Development raps a soundtrack: "Turn off your television and make way for an old vision/which will now be a new vision."

For a while Webb rides ahead with Kent, jabbering away about something, pointing at things. Whenever they reach a puddle in the road, Kent veers around while Webb steers for it. Anna pedals along yakking away with Michele and Shauna, like a little apprentice "hammerchick," as they dub her. She's keeping up a good clip with the adults, but is pedaling furiously. I'm sure she's in first gear – "It's my favorite," she tells me when I ask her why she never shifts.

New scenery today, as the road wraps around the southern point of the Island in the Sky. Ahead, in the west, is the Green River country – I haven't done much exploring on the Green River side of things. To the south, though, is the Confluence, where the Green and Colorado join and fall into the big rapids of Cataract Canyon. Sarah and I have rowed Cataract's cataracts a few times together, when ten days down the Colorado was our end-of-river-season bonus. She still married me even after I dislocated her shoulder flipping a boat down in there.

Rising in the south, above the Confluence, stands an alpine land of mountain and butte and mesa. These are the landmarks that mark my more recent years, after Sarah and I shaped a family-version of the Colorado Plateau Bum Life. The Abajos, Woodenshoe Butte, The Cheesebox, Jacob's Chair, the Sweet Alice Hills ... Sarah and I have walked and talked and driven and camped with our kids all over that landscape. Our kids have grown up thinking of the Cedar Mesa and San Juan River country as their back yard. It's just who they are.

In the afternoon, we approach one of the big ascents, the Murphy Hogback. I pull up to the first big pitch and look up and ... can't ... believe it. I get out and look, to make sure. And I'm sure: Webb is carrying Anna's bike up the hill! At home, he wouldn't carry her plate to the sink without a small fee. Sarah and the kids push their bikes the rest of the way up the narrow, absurdly steep, ridiculously rugged cliff-side trail that I now have to drive. I buckle and un-buckle the seatbelt a few times, trying to decide which would lead to the least-horrible bodily injuries were I to roll. Well, at least I'm not piloting the monster truck behind me, I think reassuringly.

After a long, slow, nervous crawl up the so-called "road," I crest the final notch in the rock and bounce onto the shelf above. I am met with the cheers of the bikers, who, I suspect, like spectators at a car race, were hoping for just a little drama. I am happy to disappoint. I run over and join my lurid friends to watch the big truck come up.

Brian's truck breeches the notch and flops down like a whale, then rolls to a rocking stop. Everyone lets out a disappointed cheer. He steps out and I hand him a beer, which he heartily accepts.

"Jesus," he says, "that was like running a waterfall in a kayak."

"Yep," I answer. "And that's how every highway pass west of Denver should be." I'm obviously one of those people.

The rest of the day is descents, and Webb and Anna ride it all. They ride until, just a few miles from camp, the storms return and hammer us with wind, lightning, and curtains of driving rain. Funny thing about the desert: the rarest of elements is also the most fearsome. Rivulets fill and flow. The road, of all times, picks now to turn down and follow a wash for a few hundred yards. We leave a wake until the road thankfully turns up onto hard ground again. As we roll on, the rain lightens, the slickrock shimmers like a silver ice sheet, and a rainbow bridges the White Rim and the Island in the Sky.

After a few miles we pull up behind the abandoned camper truck.

So we stop, get out, and wander out toward a silhouette standing on the rimrock. We meet Kent, and he points to what drew him out there: Ahead is the so-called Green River, now clay-grey and swollen with rain runoff. To our left, though, in the notch of the canyon wall, erupts a waterfall so chocolately it would make Willy Wonka lust.

Another camp. The rain has retreated. The stars burn, and we awaken to a pastel sunrise.

Our last day brings us eventually downhill to the Green River itself, where we all swim – the obligatory desert-rat ritual. We're just those kinds of people.

The kids, of course, ride their bikes. Until, that is, we reach the big switchbacking ascent up out of the canyon and back onto the Island in the Sky. We load the bikes, and Sarah and the kids climb into the truck. As we grind our way uphill, we look out over the Green River and the kids make me promise we'll soon float that unexplored part of our home.

"Okay, Dad," Anna finally declares, "it's time for our music." I knew it would happen eventually.

Sarah and I look back at our mud-covered kids jamming to No Doubt – "Hey baby, hey baby, hey!" – and grin at each other. Because now we know: They're that kind of people. Like us.

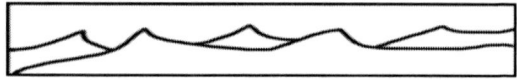

On the Road to Faith

*F*ebruary is a hard month anyway – the longest short month of the year – but this one was especially trying. Well, it happens. What happens? The usual: Loss of faith in the way the world works, personally, politically, spiritually. It's a long story, but aren't they all?

So this February I did what I usually do when I find myself in the trough of life's big waves: I loaded the truck and pointed it west. Sure, it was snowing, and pretty cold – I mean, it was February after all. And the desert very well could've been as muddy as the bottom of the Red Sea after Moses parted it. But this wasn't about rationality, prudence, practicality, or perfect conditions. All I knew was, I had to get west. So I gave a myself a simple symbolic goal: jump into the Colorado River.

First, though, I had to run the gauntlet. It should've been a simple task – purchase some bread, a can of Dinty Moore Beef Stew, and a few limes to make my cheap beer seem special. Instead, City Market turned into a nightmare run-in with the very Civilization I was fleeing.

My mistake, for even though I'd vowed never to do it, I did it anyway: in the proud American spirit of saving time, I tried the automated self-checkout. And in my weakened, faithless state, it nearly drove me mad. I stood there like Fred Flintstone trapped in a Jetson's episode, staring at this laser-beam emitting machine with its mechanical voice telling me to please put my items on the tray before me, then to plug my money into the waiting gaping slot to my right.

I just wanted some personal touch, a tiny semblance of humanity – nothing special, just a simple old checker would do. The real human, meanwhile, stood behind me, behind a desk, like an endangered species in a cage, squawking instructions from an impersonal distance. I must have looked like a moron staring back, but I was really thinking. I was thinking that she's like the once-free-ranging cowboy helping his boss string barb wire, like the windshield-washing gas-station attendant polishing the self-serve pumps, like the blue-collar factory worker voting Republican – another in a long line of American workers just doing their job, dutifully helping the economy economize themselves out of their jobs.

I bagged my own groceries and fled.

I was on my way. I could taste it. I almost made it, too, until I pulled up to the traffic light behind a shiny new $52,000 Hummer with a flag decal in the back window, and a bumper sticker that said "United We Stand." More staring and thinking. All I could think was, right now there are ten thousand camouflaged Hummers screaming across the Middle Eastern desert, making the world safe for luxury-model Hummers.

United we stand … for what? What does a Hummer stand for, anyway? United we stand about six feet off the ground in our urban assault vehicles, mo'fo! What do "we" (as in "We The People") stand for when the FBI has 80 new planes flying over the country listening in on our phone calls and taking infrared pictures of our night lives; when our e-mails are monitored for troublesome keywords that might trigger a phone tap, which is now as easy to get as a credit card; when even books you take out of the library are reported to Homeland Security?

These days, what does "security" stand for? What's the state of our "homeland"?

That's what I was going to find out. I needed to check on the security of my homeland. I needed the desert, and its green pinion and juniper rising out of red dirt. I needed the Colorado River, rain or snow and clouds and all. That was the only faith I had going for me at the time, and I was going to follow it.

West. Out through Cortez (gateway to Towaoc) until I at last reached McElmo Creek Canyon, the subtle bedrock beauty of the Hovenweep area, the rolling sandstone bluffs and sage and cottonwoods lining the shallow creek under the impeccably patient oversight of Sleeping Ute Mountain. Beauty. Across the Great Sage Plain, through the little oasis of Hatch Trading Post, and on to the highway up to Blanding, Utah, where a hand-painted sign on the side of the road announced:

*Welcome you are
entering the Ute
Indian Reservation*

Even with its cryptic grammar, I took this sign as a sign that I was headed in the right direction. I was starting to snap out of it. At times like this – personal plights, political plunder, economic entropy, ideological insanity – I turn to the land. To the sane, sensuous, bedrock reality and vitality of physical Place.

At the outskirts of Blanding, I turned left. From here on there would be few cars and minimal people, for there aren't many others nutty enough to be out here in the middle of the desert in the middle of a snowy February day. I drove on through the notch in Comb Ridge, past Grand Gulch, Natural Bridges, Sundial Butte and the Mossback Cliffs. More beauty. I turned left toward Hall's Crossing, and motored on, past the dirt road I have driven so many times down to the takeout for the San Juan River. Then the pavement begins to climb the banded redrock ridgeline called the Clay Hills. From this height I could see Monument Valley, the cavernous San Juan River country, the white fingers of Grand Gulch, and a mass of clouds swirling over where the dual buttes known as the Bears Ears – my personal spiritual epicenter – stand.

And looking out at all that, I knew it: Everything is just as it is. Everything is just as it should be. I wasn't sure what that meant, exactly. Not yet, anyway. But it didn't matter; it was what I needed to hear.

I wasn't surprised I heard that, that the land spoke to me that way. My life is written on the canyonlands. The most memorable part of it, anyway – the last half. Some of it is written in well-know spots – such as Natural Bridges National Monument, where I enjoyed a short stint as a ranger, and in canyons like Grand Gulch and Cataract and the Goosenecks—but many, many other times of my life have been marked by aimless, guide-book-less meanderings down the innumerable smaller, little-known and less-visited canyons and washes and fingers of mesa that lace this place.

All compiled, those footfalls across this landscape trace the path of my adult life. Cheesy, but there you have it. Since the early 1980s, this dry, wind-blasted, and water-scoured landscape has been my spiritual homeland. Where I find security.

Onward. Once over the Clay Hills, the road drops down onto

the big flat that spreads out toward Glen Canyon. I pulled over when I at last had a view to the stagnant water lying awkwardly, surreally, in the slickrock badland ahead of me. Somewhere there was Glen Canyon itself, one of the wonders of the world. I found, though, to my dismay although not to my surprise, that it was still submerged under Glen Canyon Reservoir. ("Lake Powell," of course, is the reservoir's marketing title, but I prefer to reserve the term "lake" for acts of gods rather than CEOs.)

I am an optimist, though, and as such, I see the canyon as half-emptied. Thanks to our Great Western Drought, the reservoir is only 50 percent full, the lowest since the concrete suppository was first inserted in Glen Canyon's bowels in the 1960s. And seeing it so low is one of the reasons I wanted to come here.

Back in the truck, and down to the Glen Canyon National Recreation Area. A mile or so from the actual boundary, a sign warned me I was about to enter "A U.S. Fee Area." The meaning, of course, is that I get to pay for access to my own land. Why not? I got to pay for its submersion, when the government built Glen Canyon Dam, to (again) help economize the economy – or at least the economies of some construction companies, power conglomerates, resort corporations, and sport boat manufacturers.

But all that so-called "improving" of our public land isn't cheap. So you and I get to pay for it, in the form of fees (now being "experimented" with as Fee Demo trail fees, but soon to be applied to all public lands). That doesn't seem to be enough, though, so now our government also wants to turn over 70 percent of Park Service jobs to private industry, have corporations such as Disney "manage" national forests, and let the oil-and-gas and logging industries make sure our public lands cough up the money they ought to. After all, something's got to pay for that nasty, expensive little war we find ourselves embroiled in, again, right? So why shouldn't our public lands do their share?

Why not? Because that's the point of public lands. Our public lands should be refuges from the cult of economics. Our public lands are not about recreation; they are about re-creation. They are national spiritual health care. They are true homeland security.

Must ... stop ... thinking, I thought to myself. I needed to get into the river.

I drove through the admission gate at the entrance to the Recreation Area – wondering how long it will be until I am greeted by a City Market-style machine, to save the cost of having a real ranger manning the booth – and headed toward the water.

The sky was clearing, against the forecasters' forecasts. In the distance, the Henry Mountains stood as a ragged line of frosted peaks sporting great hairy ice clouds. Across the water lay a tortured, rusty landscape of bare, exposed, rotten rock. Then I noticed the water itself: the floating docks sat a good 50 feet below the hanging end of the boat ramp – a steep, switch-backing, improvised footpath now led down to the water. I drove on until the very end of the road. There was the ferry, which takes travelers across the water to Bullfrog Marina, but it sat more than 100 yards from the end of the pavement. A fleet of big machinery that was working on a major extension of the enormous concrete boat ramp down to the water sat idle in the dirt.

Off to the right, I could see a huge area of hummocks and little washes, and I realized those flats of bedrock were newly exposed, seeing their first daylight in forty-some years, since they were first drowned under the stalled waters of the river. That was where I needed to go.

I left the car on the side of the road near the sleeping road-building machines, and headed off toward a little wash to the north. Once there, I found, well below the old high-water line, remnants of the reservoir's full-water glory days: a rotten Coors can, an oil funnel, plastic bags like shrunken corpses, a pair of swimming goggles.

In the bottom of the newly exposed wash, though – probably 100 feet below what was a just a few years ago the water's surface – I found deer tracks in the sand. Deer probably couldn't have reached the water here when it was flanked by bluffs; now, though, well under the white "bathtub ring" on the cliffs, deer have found again the path to the water their great-grandparents probably told them stories about.

Things are, once again, as they should be. Or are at least headed that way. Which was enough to give me faith.

I walked down to the water – still a silt-free blue from its stagnation, but Colorado River water nonetheless – peeled off my clothes, and jumped in.

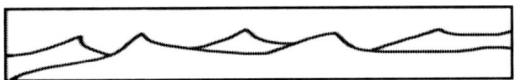

Aspen Lessons

A   *n old cabin in an aspen grove. I sit on its stone steps, facing west.*
The air chills after a hot day. The sinking sun sparkles behind
silhouettes of aspen. The western sky fades to orange. Here, on the west
slope of the Sierra La Plata, the sunsets are long and spectacular and
flaming, the days refusing to die quickly or easily.

The "here" in this passage I scribbled in the twilight more than
a decade ago is the San Juan National Forest's Aspen Guard Station.
Built by the CCC in the 1930s, the log cabin set at 9,200 feet in the
national forest served first as a ranger station, then later housed seasonal work crews until the 1970s. It sat empty and in disrepair until I
had the good fortune to be the first Artist in Residence to inhabit the
renovated log cabin. Since then, more than sixty artists have spent
time here.

I was there with Sarah, and our kids were still very young. Our
mission was to spend one week there, and I was to write about ...
well, whatever came to me by just being there.

That has been the purpose of the Aspen Guard Station Artist-
in-Residence program since its inception in 1995. Sponsored by
the San Juan National Forest and several arts groups, the program
provides a space for artists to capture, in their chosen medium, the
significance of this one little piece of our vast public lands. Several
applicants are chosen each year from a range of artists that includes
painters, writers, poets, musicians, photographers, sculptors, performers, and dancers. The artists stay for one or two weeks in the
summer, then share their art and experiences at some public venue.
They also donate a piece of their art to the Forest Service that will
serve as both record of their experience and statement of what the

forest taught them.

And what a forest it is.

One time, while Sarah and the kids lounged around the cabin, I wandered – literally, with no objective or destination – out into the vast aspen stand surrounding us. I soon picked up a drainage, first a mere southerly-tending depression in the forest floor, then a sandstone groove, then a narrow canyon that ended abruptly with a leap (the canyon, not me) off the rim of a gasp-evokingly wide, deep, and panoramic valley – the West Mancos River Canyon.

I sat down with my notebook on the edge of that abyss and savored a big drink of the expansive country: Up the valley rose the great, ragged wall of the La Plata Mountains, dominated by the banded pyramid of Hesperus Peak. At the foot of that peak, steep bedrock walls fell and funneled into the upper end of a steep gorge. From those headwaters, the Mancos River sliced into the foothill mesa country – where I sat – pouring itself downslope a few hundred feet below my perch. Following the river's route onward, my gaze turned southwesterly, where the river spilled through the town of Mancos, splayed out on the green valley floor in the distance. Then – I looked out and away now – it ran down Weber Canyon, a gap between the flat-topped Menefee Mountains and the vast escarpment of Mesa Verde, toward its remote merging with the San Juan River.

I stared. I studied. I remembered. From this vista on the very upper edge of the grand and glorious Colorado Plateau, I was able to piece together in my mental map so many familiar and beloved places, places that held so many of the stories my family and I and our tribe of friends have accumulated over so much of our lives together here. Not places, but a Place. Our Place. The Place that has made us who we are.

And we are able to have this meaningful and powerful landscape in our lives because most of what I was looking at that day is public land. Literally "our land." More than 85 percent of our southwestern Colorado home is public land. Where I sat that day is just a small part of the San Juan National Forest's 1.9 million acres spread across the western San Juan Mountains. And peering off from that perch into the distance – south to the Menefee Mountains and Mesa Verde, and to the far western horizon and beyond, where lie the magical, majestic, and varied landscapes of the Great Sage Plain, the Abajo Mountains, Elk Ridge, Cedar Mesa, and the many sculptured gorges and grottoes of the canyonlands of the Colorado and San Juan rivers – waits a vast expanse of public places managed by the Bureau of Land Management and the National Park Service. And farther, across the whole of the American West, Alaska, and in parts of the Midwest and East Coast, these government agencies (along with the U.S. Fish & Wildlife Service) oversee for us nearly 740 million of acres of land.

More than mere "land," though, these public lands are a common heritage and inheritance like that enjoyed and shared by the citizens of no other nation on earth.

But that's not what I wrote about.

After a week in the cabin in that aspen forest, I finally wrote about the many people I'd met up there enjoying and sharing the national forest: cowboys pushing cattle, locals gathering firewood, a sheepherder in his ancient wagon, horse packers, mountain bikers, ATVs on the dirt road, trucks hauling logs to the nearby sawmills, families in sedans, and hikers from everywhere from Dolores to Europe.

I also wrote about my kids.

When Sarah and I would hike with Webb and Anna around the Station, they would ride in packs on our backs. As we wandered a nearby trail one day, Webb made an imaginary phone call to his grandmother:

"'ello? … Hi damma … Hiting … Um … dees, leafs, dix, rocks, baby rocks, bir's, bu'fies, a weever, moundains, fowers …"

A pretty good inventory for a two year old. And when he wasn't in our pack, Webb was wandering – testing out those new legs – around the cabin. He didn't bother with toys; every conscious moment was filled with endless exploring, wandering his own way in these woods. His woods. And when bedtime came, he crawled merrily into his sleeping bag on the floor and fell off to sleep without a whimper.

Unstructured time in undeveloped places. Isn't this what kids crave? Require? Isn't it something all of us ache for sometime? Often?

And I came to realize that this – more than just empty, unutilized land, more than "resources" awaiting liquidation to further feed the endless hunger of the corporate industrial machine, more than some national real-estate investment portfolio to be managed for maximum immediate income, or, worse, more than some under-developed economic cash register just waiting to pander Disney

World-style to a fee-paying and entertainment-hungry public – is what our public lands have protected for the past century. Our public lands are places for everyone – not just those who can afford to pay admission, or a group with a strong enough consumer presence, or a family rich enough to buy an estate or game ranch or stretch of fishing stream – to challenge themselves, to practice their skills, to engage in self reliance, to run their own small enterprise, to get out and explore, to just … wander.

Our shared beneficence of public lands is not perfect. These places are often not economically efficient or politically logical, and managing them is usually not without its heated disagreements … but they are nonetheless ours. And they belong not just to those of us who are here now; they also are the property of those who are yet to come.

But there are those who would change that. There are those who would forget about the future to make some more bucks now. And in just the past few years, they have made great strides toward dragging our public lands into the economic maw feeding profit and short-term monetary gain – things like the opening up of nearly 90 percent of Western federal lands to oil and gas leasing, attempts to sell public lands to corporations under a 130-year-old mining law, proposals to sell off national parks to pay off the national debt, and slashing funding for land-management agencies while inviting in corporations to run these lands for profit. And lots more, every day.

Pay attention.

On our last night in the forest, I paid attention. I sat out in the dark silence and wrote a last entry in my notebook:

I scribble by flashlight, the forest still alive under the intermittent nearly-full moon, passing in and out of the day's dying summer clouds. The aspen ripple and rustle like waves on a lake – the wind made visible. A coyote yips. A satellite passes through the Big Dipper. Sarah and the kids sleep, but I cannot bear to go inside and end this night in this place.

As our national forests system limps into its second century, what I wrote about years ago is even more relevant today than it was then: How our national forests, and all our public lands, are an investment in national spiritual healthcare, places set aside so all Americans can afford to get out, to get close to the land. Places for anyone of any economic means or social class to find a Place. And how they are places held in trust for our children and their children – people who will need these places even more than we do now.

That's what my time among the aspen taught me.

Among
The Tribe

All the freaky people make the beauty of the world.
Michael Franti

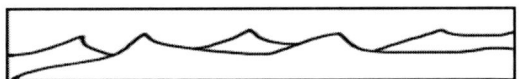

San Juan Shangri-la

*I*t was a dream-like day. Or maybe it a day-like dream. Either way, it seemed I suddenly found myself in a truck creeping up a muddy single-lane mountain road gouged between tall, overshadowing snowbanks. It was early morning. I lifted my head out of the truck's sunroof, filling my nose with scents of decaying ice and the leaking, sappy life-blood of the broken, dismembered trunks and limbs of trees that had been swept down in the many avalanches lacing the valley. These brittle sticks were now sticking out from the snow-corridor's walls in dark, bony fragments. Foreboding fragments, for over the rim of the snow-cut I could see fresh spring sloughs and slides laid over the rough remnants of the season's older killers.

Then we were on skis, and hauling backpacks full of camping gear. Ahead lay a snow-filled valley like a Pleistocene playground, a craggy mountainscape of unbroken snow. Which seemed crazy, even to my sleepy (or sleeping?) mind. It's mid-May, right? Just last weekend I was luxuriating on a hot desert river trip, no? But my "real world" mind and memories had no role here. The sky was a depthless oceanic blue, the sun surreal and piercing. We trudged upward along a long ski track – following others? All I knew was to follow my companions, expecting they knew where we were headed.

Miles. We came to a division in the ancient glacial valley. Decaying, sunburnt buildings stood half-buried in the lingering snowpack. Above us here, too, fresh avalanches like upside-down mushroom clouds lay splayed and splattered, falling out of cirques and couloirs, and superimposed on top of older, deeper remnants of even more explosive snowslides.

My friends chose the left valley, where thousand-foot white-walled ramparts marched away out of sight over a crisp rounded rise in the valley floor. We slid on, across the snow, up the hill, until we crested the rise. And there we saw it.

I'd heard stories about such a place. There are tales of such mythic spots the world over – Shambhala ... Shangri-La ... Brigadoon ... El Dorado – those ethereal, ephemeral, egalitarian kingdoms where gather peaceful warriors for rituals, celebrations, renewal, rejoicing, and challenges. Places that then fade back into the landscape, protected by the earth, clothed in some sort of magical cloaking, until the tribe meets again, conjuring the kingdom back into existence, for a time.

And I'd heard the tales of our own version of such a power spot in our own beloved San Juans. Many late nights around pool tables under smoky lights in local bars, and around flaming campfires, and on chairlift rides, and on long mountain walks, I've been told the fables of the village that appears dream-like in the snow high in the ragged San Juan spires. There, it is said, a warrior society of snow stalkers gathers and rallies to share and shred the surrounding snowfields for a time. And then the tribe disperses and the snow-village fades away, for a time.

Shangri-la in the San Juans.

In fact, I'd heard just such a legend the night before, from the two friends who have appeared here in this dreamscape ski with me. I'd heard that the encampment had been seen again, up north, up high, up some forgotten and forlorn glacier-scoured, rock-strewn, snowfield-patched and avalanched-scarred mountain valley. Like this one.

And there it was. Surreal. Dreamy. Mirage-like. Somehow archaic and modern at the same time – instead of brick or stone or log, a canvas kingdom of orange dome tents of various sizes rising like colorful bubbles from the whitewash of the valley floor. Excited, we floated on our skis – in the way that dreams let you convert your awe and desire directly to motion – down the hill and into camp. We were welcomed by two guards who pointed us to one of the many lodges arrayed in the snow. We dropped our gear. They asked us to make an offering. And in the spirit of warrior kinship – of the ski-bum kind of warrior – they in turn offered us beer.

We felt we were meant to be here.

And we were meant to be up there. I looked up and around and noticed for the first time that the slopes – all the alluring, enticing, rising and gleaming fall lines around us – were marked with the meandering tracks of descending skis. We needed to go. So we went.

We climbed, pulling ourselves up drainages and slopes and ridges and headwalls. For hours, it seemed. Or minutes, it may have been. Or a full lifetime. It's hard to know in those dream places, where time's true nature is revealed: just a dead memory-record of the path of the flow of the living and glowing moments that are the only real reality – like the difference between the trip itself and the odometer that measures it. In dreamspaces, as it should be all the time, perhaps, it's the flashing of the moments and not their mental afterglow that we should attend to.

We climbed farther, higher, steeper. I was winded and worked and wickedly, wonderfully happy when we reached to top and stopped and looked around. Ahead stood a horizon of great, glistening peaks like quartz shards. Then I noticed that there were, on every slope, others like us, like slow-moving blips on a radar screen wending their way up or meandering their way down in wide free-falling turns, unreeling behind them sine-wave-shaped mountain-side line art.

It was time to carve our own. One by one, we pushed off and dropped over the edge of the abyss. The wide white fell away before me, and I fell onto it, with only my skill and style and resolve keeping me from falling into it. The spilling of corn ice crystals glissading down the near-sheer slope below me sounded like a stream as my skis rode the flow.

Hours later, back in camp, the sun sunken, the warriors re-gathered. The scene was outlandish, even for a dream – a kitchen the size of a bus had been carved into the snowpack, complete with ice tables and shelves. A snow-block wall held a well-stocked bar. And in a packed-down common area, a rendezvous was under way: dozens from disparate tribes, represented by their colorful collage of ski gear, circled together, all drinking and laughing and spouting loud, animated, gesticulating renderings of the day's epics and adventures and experiences and views and visits, like Vikings or pirates or explorers or braves back from their wild forays.

And as high-country twilight lapsed into a star-strewn and moon-lit night, as the gathered snow-worshippers grew familiar with each other – and as the bond of honor forged on shared risk, challenge, and beauty morphed into celebration and comraderie – the magic of the mythic and mysterious warrior kingdom was once again unleashed, in its own, unique San Juan Mountain way.

A banquet emerged from the snow-kitchen: a platter the size of the hood of a car covered with fresh sushi was served by a tiny, cheery Thai chef in Sorels. Glowing flying disks streaked over camp. Sledders in the moonlight launched themselves down slopes and off ramps. The burning effigy of a popular cartoon character lifted one selected burden – written on a scrap of paper and tossed into the flames – from the mind of each participant.

This is a good dream, I thought to myself as, after hours it seemed, I snuck away. I knew that it was ending – that, soon, after the revelers had returned to their own clans, the snow-carved camp would melt away, dissolving back into memory and story, like a sand painting. Or that this dream, if that's all it was, would slip away from the grasp of my myth-making mind.

But I didn't want to forget. So I vowed, as I crawled into my moon-glowing dome in middle of this transitory mountain village, that when I woke up – where ever I found myself waking up – I would write this tale down.

And that's what I did.

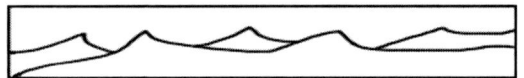

Among the Tribe

So there we were, sitting in the dark and the cold, surrounded by a couple hundred other folks in lawn chairs. We were all there to "watch" speakers we could not see, because it was dark and there were no lights. An oversight, it seems. And it was cold, because it was night in the mountains outside of Moab, even though it had been a lovely spring afternoon. It probably would've been best to start the event – since it included a dozen speakers – at, like, 1 p.m., when it was warm and lovely. And light. A misjudgment, it would appear.

But I'm not complaining. And I wasn't complaining even then, when my wife and I were sitting in the cool spring blackness, just listening. Even though you could argue this was a poorly planned event, I was loving it, because, I ask, is this not The Tribe? Kind of half-assed but well-intentioned. Half-baked but somehow still well done. To me, The Tribe has always seemed, like its esteemed figurehead, philosophical and fun even amidst its perfect imperfection. Such is the Buddha-nature of both Edward Abbey and The Abbey Tribe.

My wife and I had come to the Pack Creek Ranch to see some of my heroes – elders in the tribe – as they gathered outside Moab for a sort of radical environmental version of a classic rock reunion tour. Abbey (isn't it interesting that he is recognized by just one name, like he's the West's Elvis or Sting or Ringo?) spent a lot of time living, writing, and exploring here. In memoriam, the few roads crossing the ranch today reference Abbey's works, with names such as Seldom Seen Road, Abbey Road, and Take The Other Road.

This gathering was billed as "Ed Abbey Speaks," a reunion of Abbey's closest entourage, commemorating the 15th anniversary of his death. (And also, appropriately, the 40th anniversary of the Wilderness Act.) Making the event even more momentous, this was very likely the last-ever gathering of some of the eldest of the elders in the tribe. These flower children have long since gone to seed – but isn't that what flowers do after they bloom? Spreading seeds is just another vital stage of life, and the two hundred or so of us came here to gather those vital seeds.

The event was a fundraiser for the Glen Canyon Institute, a nonprofit with the mission of, essentially, keeping alive the memory of the still-wild Glen Canyon, while endeavoring to convince the world it ought to be restored – Abbey's personal jihad brought to the organizational level. And with Glen Canyon Reservoir at only 42 percent full – 58 percent empty! – now's the time to decommission the dam, and to create Abbey's long longed-for Floyd Dominy Falls, an appropriate memorial to the Bureau of Reclamation commissioner who backed the dam. And perhaps it's a tribute to the spreading of Abbey's seeds that before the speakers began, my wife and I spied, milling about amidst us spectators, another former BuRec commissioner, chatting with a small group sporting "Damn Dam" hats.

Seeds are amazing things. Especially when they're weed seeds.

As the sun set downvalley – taking with it our light and heat – we moved onto the little meadow behind a huge campfire and in front of the lodge and log outbuildings. A lovely little ridge lined with cottonwoods ran alongside us and away to the west, where the sinking sun burned a brilliant hole in the sky. People – ranging from crusty Utahn old timers, to middle-aged "enviromeddlers," as Abbey called us activists, to young couples with their tooling toddlers – sat in lounge chairs and Crazy Creeks next to coolers, like a 200-person river trip. Behind us the La Sals rose Alpishly, with – an amazing and blessed thing on May 1 – its snowpack still unbroken down into and below treeline.

Festivities began with the awarding of the David Brower Award. This year's goes to Kent Frost, a long-time canyonlands backcountry guide from Monticello who, along with his wife, Fern, nearly single handedly got Canyonlands National Park created. Kent is now 84, as thin and sun-baked as an old juniper snag. He shuffled his way up to the front, held the microphone before him like it was a weird alien artifact, weakly cleared his throat in front of the silent crowd, then, apparently wasting no time embracing his role as tribal elder, he spoke in a startlingly strong voice: "What we need to do is …"

Frost was followed by a brief introduction of the rest of the speakers by Dave Wegner, world-renowned river activist and member of the Glen Canyon Institute's board of directors. "We want to bring to you a sense of Ed," Wegner explained, "and a sense of what's really important." Are those things one in the same? Here, tonight: Yes. In this tribe: Yes. And to nutshell those things, Wegner began the night by playing a song from the new CD from musician Tom Russell, a song titled "The Ballad of Edward Abbey." "If a man can't piss in his own front yard," sang Russell, quoting Abbey, "he's living too close to town."

And away we went.

The first speakers knew Abbey as well as anybody. David Petersen, a friend in the last years of Abbey's life and the steward of his literary estate, led off. Gray-bearded (this seemed to be a theme among the speakers) and sporting an olive-drab shirt and grinning under a ball cap, he read excerpts from Abbey's journals, and then marveled over the power of even that casual prose. Abbey's truest gift? "He gave voice to the passion and love of natural beauty that we all feel, but can't say," Petersen offered.

But Abbey was no guru, Petersen continued, attacking the recent – and inevitable – wave of academic analyses of Abbey's works and life. "Don't deconstruct the myth! He was flawed!" he pleaded. "He was one of us ... and we need our heroes."

Ken Sleight followed, but slowly. Already well-along in years, Sleight got pretty busted up from a fall off a horse recently, a gaffe for which he was acutely embarrassed. With his years of experience horseback riding and guiding as owner of Pack Creek Ranch, he claimed he should've known better. "My dad tells me I was conceived on a horse," ho joked. "That's a hell of a long time ago, right?" Sleight met Abbey after he wrote him a fan letter following reading *Desert Solitaire*. Their friendship was solidified, Sleight explained in a rambling reminiscence, by the years they spent together right there at the ranch. Sleight eventually became the model for Seldom Seen Smith, in *The Monkey Wrench Gang*.

The river trip atmosphere grew as the night grew darker. I pulled on my thick 1970s Patagonia jacket and some fingerless gloves. As the sun waned, the nearly-full moon gained strength over the alpenglowing La Sals. A poorwill hooted from the cottonwoods nearby (poor Will!). As I pulled out my notebook to take notes, I set my beer down into a pile of deer shit.

Is this perfect for our tribe, or what? Who needs lights, heat, as-signed seating, careful planning? Give us alpenglow and moonlight, birdsong and cottonwood canopy, a lawn chair and deer scat for my cup holder. Gritty? Yes. Flawed? Fuck, yes!

Bart Kohler, co-founder of Earth First! and long-time eco-bard singing under the pseudonym Johnny Sagebrush, livened things up with a musical set that included such tribal classics as "Were you there when they killed the river?" and "The Monkey Wrench Song." This was followed by the joyous, bountiful, distinct laughter and tale-telling of Abbey comrade and biographer Jack Loeffler. Ed's greatest accomplishment was "to live out who he really was," Loeffler prof-fered. "A hand-crafted life."

It struck me as interesting how this theme – how Abbey lived as a man, as a person, how his was a life lived – was as common a topic this night as the eco-messages Abbey is so renown for outside the tribe. Yet as much an eco-visionary and gifted writer as Abbey was, like David Petersen said, he was flawed – multiple divorcee, financial bottom-dweller, and equal-opportunity insuler. Yet within the tribe he is a hero, as Petersen also noted, for his spirit, for his art-of-living. What's up with that?

Milagro Beanfield War author John Nichols took the mike next (from what I could hear since it was too dark to see). Nichols spent the first minutes talking about his recent open-heart surgery – an-other sign of the aging of the elders. When he finally got around to talking about Abbey, he pointed out that despite years of correspon-dence he only actually spent one hour in Abbey's presence. "But I felt after that I could write a novel about him," he said. And what would the character in that novel be like? Nichols gave an example: After a severe heart attack in 1989, Abbey wrote Nichols a long, sincere, and reflective letter, sympathizing and empathizing with Nichols' brush with mortality by discussing the experiences of and thoughts on his own long-time illness. This was an act of great compassion that Nichols felt helped him rally to recover. Then he found out how deathly ill Abbey himself was when he wrote the letter: Abbey was dead within a couple of weeks.

Other speakers took turns, rising (I assume) and offering their thoughts and memories of Abbey: Bob Lippman, a lawyer friend Ab-bey consulted when he was composing *Hayduke Lives!* ... River rat, folk singer, and author Katie Lee (the sexiest 83-year-old woman I've ever met) ... Publisher Ken Sanders, who struggled to read some e.e.

cummings by headlamp light … Howie Wolke, another co-founder of Earth First! (whom I had never actually seen speak in person, and, I guess, still haven't), whose speech was the most academic and monotone, but who also offered perhaps the most insightful and visionary words: that Abbey believed it was vital to keep the idea of Wilderness alive as much as real wilderness. It's essential for humanity, he said, summarizing a conversation he had with Abbey, that we work to resist the slow de-evolution of the notion of wilderness and wildness – what he called "wilderness amnesia" over generations – by keeping alive the vision of wilderness in its "most elemental, uncompromised form."

Then another musician, Bob Greenspan, played his song that was made famous in an Abbey essay: "Big Tits, Braces, and Zits." (Soooo flawed!) And the evening ended, as so many Abbey Tribe rallies have ended for the past 25 years, with Dave Foreman (an eco-hero in his own right) leading his trademark crowd-wide wolf howling. "I'm cold, you're cold. I'm in the dark, you're in the dark," he observed appreciatively. But his voice, as always, lit up the night.

So, that was it. It was over.

It was late by then, and damn cold, and still dark despite the moon's best efforts at playing stand-in for the sun. We folded up our lawn chairs, felt around in the dark for empties and tossed them into our cooler, and fumbled our way back to our camping spot – my van was parked near the corner of Pack Creek and Desert Solitaire roads. The Great Reunion was over … and what did it all mean? In retrospect, there was no theme, no great single Abbey Idea that came out of it all. Wouldn't a well-planned event have had a pointed agenda? This, though, was just a lot of memories, reflections, observations, celebrations, invocations …

But so what? This was another flaw – and another perfect imperfection. For what was really important was the gathering itself. That it happened, again. What mattered most was just The Tribe. The Spirit.

And what is that spirit? Not a plan, nor a program, and neither organization nor incorporation of any sort. (Which is not to say that groups like the Glen Canyon Institute aren't important.) But the spirit of this night was more akin to Earth First! – and I mean the original manifestation of Earth First!, the disorganization that was Earth First! in the 1980s. Back then, in its early incarnation, the way founders Foreman, Wolke and Kohler envisioned it – and lived it when those flower children where blooming – Earth First! was a vision, an intuition, a connection, a sensibility. And to be an "Earth First!er" meant absolutely nothing about dues, membership, or rosters; it meant simply the agreed-upon guiding principle (manifested in as many ways as there are adherents) that Nature is going to, as always, eventually take care of our careless issues – there is no evidence of anything else in history, biology, or ecology – so we may as well make good decisions now, while we still have some things left. We may as well save some wildness, both terrestrial and human, while there's some to save. We may as well put the Earth first (And may as well do that with an exclamation point). And to be an Earth First!er meant, as Foreman reiterated that night, to "stand up and do something in both joy and defiance."

And that – joy and defiance, a most perfectly imperfect combination – is the spirit of Abbey. And of the Abbey Tribe.

The next morning, Sarah and I got up well before the sun scaled the great wall of the La Sals. We brewed strong coffee, then took a walk, drinking our coffee, saying little, letting the morning speak. We wandered up Desert Solitaire Road toward those so-close peaks.

And what did we see? It was like a parody: survey stakes and flagging, brand-new water taps and electrical boxes and fire hydrants, and bulldozers and gouged driveways and freshly scraped building lots. That's right: as soon as we got above Pack Creek Ranch, we walked right into – what the fuck else? – "Desert Solitaire Subdivision." Complete with one completed model house: a big, glassy, adobe trophy, which could be ours for just $798,000, alongside a few dozen other soon-to-be second homes crammed into the little rolling pinion-juniper foothills lining Abbey's beloved Pack Creek.

Welcome to our 21st Century reality: Realty First! "The turning of the screw," as Abbey liked to say …

So, I thought sarcastically, angrily, suffering: Could Abbey still piss in his front yard here?

I chewed on this bitter pill for a while, trying to wash it down with long draws on my coffee, wondering what it all means, what the

hell good all this blather about the Abbey Spirit is worth …
    And then it hit me: Could Abbey still piss in his front yard here?
No matter: *He still would've.* In joy and defiance.
    And that's why we were there.

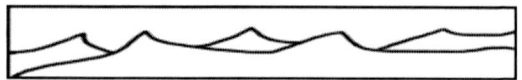

My Life in the Bar of Bums

*M*y life changed in the Crooked Creek Saloon. Several times.

Once upon a time, I walked away from a perfectly good professional and personal life in Boston, and walked into an impoverished life of manual labor among strangers. I became a ski bum in Colorado's Fraser River Valley. I had no plan, vision, program or agenda. I had traded a good job, nice girlfriend, comfortable apartment, and a new sofa for, essentially, just hanging around in a beautiful, snow-filled mountain valley, learning to ski, driving a bus for a ski pass, and having fun just for the sake of having fun while ... well, whatever was to happen as a result of that decision happened.

And a lot of it happened, or was celebrated after it happened, in the Crooked Creek Saloon, in Fraser, Colorado.

After a few weeks in the Winter Park Youth Hostel, the first place I settled into was the brand new, first-of-its-kind-in-the-valley, modern-style, papier-mâché-and-toothpick-quality condo complex along the Fraser River, and across the street from the Crooked Creek Saloon. Hence, my first celebration: My three condo-mates and I headed for our new-neighborhood's nearby tap.

We found a good omen: Our first visit to the Creek happened to be on a 25-cent draw night, also known, we would learn, as "Wednesday Night at the Fights." And so began several years worth of Wednesday nights, and other nights, at the Creek.

I never got into a fight there, although I saw some, such as they were. Most were silly affairs – some pushing at the crowded bar, like a mini Who concert, for a slot among the barstool squatters through which to order another round. Some grumbling and slurred slurs, mostly. I don't remember anything ever coming to actual, sincere, heart-felt blows, and I think that's because frequenting a small bar in a small town is like pitching in the National League: there's that respectful understanding that you're going to have to step into the batter's box against – or stand at the urinal alongside – that person again, so you might think twice about hitting him intentionally.

No, the Creek was not about fights. It was more about convivial festiveness, good-natured razzing, happy buzzes, and some dancing. The dance floor was small – not that the Creek didn't pack to standing-room-only for the weekend bands, but, pragmatically, the limiting variable in dance-floor need was the low number of women available. Which also defined the area's singles scene: The saying in the Fraser Valley was that when you broke up with someone you didn't lose a love, you just lost a turn.

Nonetheless, dancing at the Creek did mark another first for me: It was, and remains, the only place where I have danced in front of a hundred people with a professional belly dancer. I'm not sure why there was a belly dancer in the Crooked Creek on one of those 25-cent draw nights, but one Wednesday night, there she was, with bells jingling and colorful scarves writhing around a low blouse and swaying skirt. I may never know what karmic forces brought her to my little table in the middle of the crowded room, but she homed on a trajectory my way until she stood shimmying in front me. While I attempted to focus on the jiggling blur of her bare belly, she reached out and lifted me by my flannel shirt with only a single digit, like one of those women who lifts a collapsed car off her trapped husband. And then I danced.... .

That's the first time I knew I would not be returning to Boston.

There were other firsts there, too. In fact, it's where I first saw the woman who would become my wife. When I met her, I was there with my girlfriend of the time, but I was soon to lose my turn – she ended up betraying me, and The Creek, by leaving me for the bartender at another, newer bar "up the valley," in Winter Park. But before she left me, she introduced me to Sarah.

Sarah was a standout in the Crooked Creek's female lineup. She was seated at the bar, holding a Bud longneck provocatively and looking young and lovely and intriguing. She also had – this was the mid 1980s mind you – her head shaved in a broad band just above her ears and below a mass of flaming red hair. This was, let's say, "distinctive" in a bar full of cowboys, river rats, powder hounds and construction workers. It wasn't love at first sight – we only mumbled "nice't'meetya"s as I dutifully followed my soon-to-be-ex girlfriend to a table – but I certainly remembered her. It was love at second sight, though, a few months later, when I got my turn.

Sarah and I had our first dates at the Creek, drinking beers and sipping tequila while my redneckness and her New Wave-ism found common ground in our ski-bum lives. Over the years of courtship that followed, we had other firsts there, too: We withstood our first test there, when, on one of those crazy, spinning last days of the ski season, another couple tried to pick us up. Later still, after we had moved out of the valley, we took a detour to celebrate the conclusion of a long road trip with a visit to the Creek, where she got me drunk and convinced me it was time to have a kid.

What first hooked us, and kept us returning to the Creek, was not each other, though. It was our fellow Creekers. The Creek worked miracles of peacemaking that would make Jimmy Carter weep. At the Crooked Creek gathered an oddly, almost bizarrely, diverse group of folks – Eastern transplants and life-long mountain men (and women) and Bronco-fan construction workers and Kiwi world travelers and tent-dwelling hippies and fly-fishing zealots and other outcasts from the Real World – who merrily gathered together in a loose, alcohol-lubed solidarity on the West Slope of the Bell Curve.

My most memorable of those unlikely alliances was with DJ (not his real initials, to protect the guilty). Descended from a Fraser Valley pioneer family, DJ and I bonded, Colorado cowboy and Boston ski bum, when we spent a night systematically extinguishing the dozen-or-so streetlights blurring the view of the moon-lit Continental Divide from our mountain-hamlet neighborhood. We were a good team: I carried the slingshot and DJ carried a small keg, from which we toasted each kill. We had found our shared religion, and we cemented that devotion over shards of glass.

What really endeared me to DJ, though, was his almost paleolithic presence in the modern world, best illustrated, perhaps, with an event that occurred just outside the Crooked Creek's back door. This particular night it was snowing one of those dense, steady snowfalls that blessed the Colorado high country so often in the early '80s. I was driving my night-time bus route, which brought me every hour to a stop sign across the highway from the Creek, where my headlights beamed into the lot behind the bar. Midway through that night, on one of my stops at the corner of County Road 8 and U.S. 40, I could see something through the nearly opaque snowfall, lying behind the Creek like an enormous abandoned football.

Next hour, next time at the stop sign, I could see something else. Like an image through bad TV reception, I thought I could make out a circle of figures huddled around the mega-pigskin-like thing. Next hour, same view, but this time ... something was still there, but the figures were gone, and the "football" looked deflated. It was nearly midnight by then, and my bus empty, so this time I checked it out. I pulled across the highway and behind the bar until my high beams illuminated the mystery mound: Lying there in the snow was the carcass of a horse, or what was left of it, wearing only a sheer veneer of snow for skin.

The next day, over a beer and a shot, DJ explained. Late that previous night, DJ's horse, which he had ridden, as he often did, to the Crooked Creek to avoid DUIs, had gotten loose and been hit by the train. Upon hearing the news, and while his dead partner was still warm, he and his cowpoke comrades went out in the snow and skinned the horse, so DJ could make a jacket to honor his fallen friend. They then headed back in to celebrate the passing.

So, what did an ex-pat from the Red Sox Nation like myself have in common with a Colorado cowpoke like DJ? Or, for that matter, with all the other unlikeliest of people and crowds at the Creek, people I would have never approached, never mind befriended, in my old urban life – cabin-dwelling granolas, the "Flying A's" softball team (and the "A" wasn't for "Athletics," as indicated on their hats, which bore an orifice-like circle with three streamers coming out of the hole), country-swinging Andy, country-music-picking Gary (whose turn was before mine with my first Valley girlfriend), beautiful Amazon Heidi, the loveliest of hard-ass waitresses Nancy and Kathy, River Rat Mike 1 and River Rat Mike 2, and many, many others. What deep, underlying thread was spun in the smoky, loud, sticky, stinky, wooden-walled and linoleum-floored confines of the Crooked Creek Saloon?

I don't think I could have answered that question back then. It was just what we did ... it was just what we were doing. Now, though, that my life is a bit more "real" – I have a house, a family, a job or two – I find that much of who I am today was found, forged and formulated in the Crooked Creek Saloon. So I would now like to venture an explanation for the Creek's alchemy:

As disparate and dissimilar a clientele as we were, we were all, in one way or another, each in his or her own way, bums. My dictionary defines "bum" as, "A worthless or dissolute loafer." True enough. From the inside, though, from the view of being a "bum," that same definition would be offered, but with a tone of pride, joy, satisfaction, and thirst. "Worthless" and "dissolute"? Yes! That's why we valued 25-cent beer! "Loafers"? Fuck, yes! It's what we aspired to! That's why we were living in the mountains! "Bum" was our shared, unifying vision. It was our mood, spirit, attitude of living rather than any particular way of "making" that living. We all agreed on how we wanted to live; and we all in unison, regardless of how we got there, agreed on why we were living that way. Because it was interesting, challenging, unpredictable, sensuous, tangible, visceral. Not a living, but living itself.

And, hence, that was the spirit we conjured with each other and for each other in that sacred space spontaneously generated nightly in the Crooked Creek Saloon. I even propose a technical term for a congregation of these creatures: Like a murder of ravens, a gaggle of geese, a pod of whales, I would call it a bar of bums. Add that to your field guide to Rocky Mountain wildlife.

So now, somewhere way down the path of that bum living, I can safely say that the Creek got me where I am today: a more "real" life, for sure, but still in that bum style: still with no career, still working odd jobs, still calling in sick for powder days (and now calling my kids in sick to school for powder days), still married to Sarah, and, as soon as I finish typing this story, I'm still walking to town to join my neighborhood bar of bums.

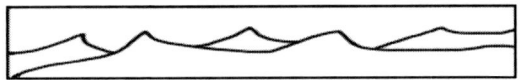

Eracism
Touching a touchy subject

*O*ur first night was welcoming.

After we got our gear settled into the youth center, we drove down to the casino, where the Tribe was holding a pageant and dance. This was not a tourist show. A log shelter covered a circular dirt dancing area surrounded by a ring of benches. Tribal members sat in the bleachers and on blankets spread on the grass outside the shelter. Kids chased each other while adults hunched and talked. A concession sold snacks and drinks. The casino blinked its neon luminescence over our shoulders, but no one inside gambled on leaving the gaming for this event. The big mountain that loomed over the little town faded to grey silhouette in the pastel sunset.

Our group of more than two dozen arrived in a string, weaving ourselves into the intimate gathering. Things were already underway. Up front, a table of judges sat watching a young boy in ornate "Fancy Dancer" regalia as he trotted a swinging, spinning dance to a deep drum beat. After that, a series of other dancers – several young women, another couple of children – did the same, each dancer with their own style and look, each dance with its own accompanying tune, pounded out by the four men seated around a big drum.

We were the only non-Indians there. The kids we were with – 26 8th-grade students from San Francisco – watched tentatively, some standing, some sitting, drinking it in, whispering to each other occasionally, pointing here and there.

After the performances, awards were issued – several of the dancers were chosen as that year's young ambassadors to represent the Tribe. Then elders, sitting in a folding-chair row behind the MC, were recognized, each individually named, followed by inside jokes that sparked ripples of chuckling throughout the crowd. The warmth of the community radiated like the desert releasing the day's heat back to the night.

"We'd like to welcome the students from San Francisco," the MC said to the crowd unexpectedly. We hadn't told anyone here who we were. Heads nodded all around us, looking our way. It was obvious which were us. "They'll be staying with us for a few days." More somber nodding.

"Maybe later," the MC continued, addressing us after a short pause, "you can dance like Indians."

The crowd laughed out loud, casting more glances at us. Jono, Fritz, and I, three of the five trip leaders, laughed, too. We'd been there before. We knew the desert-dry nature of Native humor – myself, I find it akin to that acerbic New England bantering that I had to curtail when I moved West because nobody got it out here. Not everyone got this joke, either. Three students standing near us, faces pinched as this was going on, turned to us: "Are they making fun of us?" one asked.

"They just welcomed us," Jono explained.

But their confusion only grew, I'm sure, when after a few more formal dances, the MC invited the spectators to join in, again speaking directly to his non-Native guests:

"Come out!" he implored. None of our students moved, which seemed only to challenge him. "Come out!" he entreated us again, "Come make a circle. It's just like circling the wagons when the Indians are going to attack!"

The Indian audience about fell off their seats laughing at this one, while our students stared, patently uncertain about what was transpiring around them.

But a few believed that what they were seeing and hearing was okay, and tentatively entered the ring. Several of the dancers already getting into place greeted and guided them into spaces in the two concentric circles that were forming. And when the drumming started again, we watched our students lose their initial awkwardness and soon find their stride, stepping and flowing with the rhythmic roll of the circles.

ın—

This, of course, was why we were there. This week-long trip around the Four Corners was a sort of rite of passage to prepare these students for that bigger, more challenging world awaiting them in high school. I was there as a guide for the tour company hired to lead this entourage on this combination of adventure and service work that, we hoped, would give them a quick but meaningful taste of the delicious smorgasbord of land and people that is southwestern Colorado.

On this trip already, they'd run a river, climbed a mountain, and done service work with the Forest Service. This visit to the Ute Mountain Ute Tribe, though, was something new and alien, even for this group's cultural, racial, social and economic stew – as it was, I'm sure, for Towaoc's residents, who, aside from trolling for dollars with the Ute Mountain Casino, do not pander to tourists or visitors. And while other school and church groups visit and do service work with the tribe, our school group – this was the second year in a row they came here – was, we had been told, the only group to actually stay in Towaoc.

The next day followed in the positive wake carved by that first welcoming night. Our group went into the Ute Mountain Tribal Park to visit the ancient cliff dwellings and to work clearing out two 800-year-old check dams that had filled with sediment after last year's fires. Our two Ute guides kept us entertained with history and stories and humor and spontaneous Ute language lessons. The students worked hard moving dirt and clearing brush and were appreciative of the history and their presence in this rugged, remote, silent canyon.

The next morning, the students spun off into teams to tackle more service projects. Jono and I took a group out to the end of a long and lonely dirt road at the base of Sleeping Ute Mountain to re-paint the faded face of a tribal elder's house. Another team spent the morning at the Head Start school, where they did some maintenance work and played and read with the kids. A third group organized a series of games and activities for the community-wide gathering scheduled for the town park that afternoon to celebrate the last day of school for Towaoc's students.

This event would transform their experience.

It began well enough: our students ran around and played games with the little kids they'd met earlier that day. Meanwhile, we adults talked with the teachers, tribal staffers, and parents over hamburgers and hot dogs and sodas. Through the afternoon, more kids arrived – the middle schoolers, and, finally, the high school kids.

I cannot say how or when or why the fabric of the event deteriorated, but unravel it did. Suffice to say that by the end of the day, words had been exchanged, slurs had been chalked onto a picnic table, and even a couple of us adults had been thrown the universal single-digit anti-greeting by some of the older local kids. A dark mood fell over the picnic, and soon everyone moved on, and we corralled our students into the youth center.

Damage control. The chaperoning teachers held a debriefing circle with the students to deflect the retaliatory anger, to defuse the confusion and cheap categorization, to deconstruct the experience and wring out some significance. And on the outside of our enclave, we knew the Ute adults were doing something similar with other kids.

And myself? Listening to this meeting, I was thinking … *This stuff happens.*

I know that's not very reassuring, or sensitive, or creative, or liberal, or assertive, or profound. But that's how I feel about this: that this came to pass is not a surprise. It's not what I wanted to have happen, or think should have happened; but it also is not a surprise. This is not meant as any kind of judgment against the Ute kids or the San Francisco kids or kids in general or anyone else. Because … this stuff happens everywhere.

Here's what I wanted to prance around and blurt out like some whacked street-corner preacher at the debriefing: We all have our favorite graven image of who's going to give us grief, whether that portrait is painted in to highlight a skin color, income level, social situation, or cultural category. But the fact is, in my four and a half decades of traveling around, I've had run ins with someone, some people, in damn near every group I've ever encountered. Not just those obviously different from me; I've been hassled by prim college professors, businessmen and professional women, mountain bikers, river runners, college students, and pasty-white trust-fund skateboard punks in downtown Telluride.

Even though I didn't voice my view, Jono offered a story at the debriefing that illustrated this point: "Look, I am as heterosexual as they come. But when I first moved to San Francisco," he said, bringing his point literally home to this group – and it should be noted here that Jono has bleached-white hair and sports two large silver loop earrings – "one of my first experiences was to get called 'fag'. In San Francisco!"

His real point came after, though, when he laughed, hard, and just shrugged.

This stuff happens. These people exist. Everywhere. Is this just the way we work? The way humans are wired? I don't believe that, either – not individually, anyway. But as I see it, within the bell curve of any population, there are cooperative, curious, welcoming people; and there are mean, defensive, aggressive people; and there are hurt, suffering, confused and abused people. And we cannot know, or pretend to know, the backstory that has led any person or group of people to where they lash out in the way they do or for the reasons they do.

This may not be part of being human, but it is part of the greater human landscape, as much as thunderstorms or floods or droughts are part of the land. Just as random. Just as predictable. Just as un-avoidable. And sometimes just as dangerous. We're not going to change that. Or understand that. Or deconstruct that. But: we can control how we react. We always, no matter what, control our own attitude.

I never jumped up and offered my lecture though. The meeting ended, with a fair share of tears and grumblings, but overall every-one seemed better for it.

As the kids filed out of the room toward their sleeping bags, Jono stood next to me. "We wanted to expand their minds," he said, "and they got exploded."

The next day, before we left, several people, adults and kids, came by to see us, to talk, to blow on the coals of our friendship. One woman, a mother of one of the local kids involved, gave one of our involved students a necklace so she'd remember what was and should be honored as the true experience there.

"It's going to take time to earn their trust," Fritz said as we were loading the vans. "Until then, I can see why they'd see us as a bunch of tourists come to gawk at the Indians."

Meanwhile, a half dozen of our students were over hanging with a dozen or more kindergarten-age kids on the swing set, laughing and yakking and chasing each other around. They weren't, I was thinking as I watched them, exhibiting mere "tolerance," or even practicing Zen-ish "acceptance"; they were fully appreciating each other. Sharing. Exploring. Just being with each other.

Fritz pointed at them. "They'll have good memories of us to start with, if nothing else," he said.

The students were returning to San Francisco the next day, so we had one more stop on their Four Corners cultural journey. We drove the two hours from Towaoc to Ignacio to spend the day at the Southern Ute Bear Dance Powwow.

This event would transform our experience, again.

Colors. People wearing a dizzying, dazzling array of colors, cut and worn in infinite variety. Spinning and moving and flowing. And drum-pounding so pulsing and penetrating that it beat my heartbeat into step.

I don't come to a powwow to gawk. I come to be there.

The students were fully there as well, visibly soaking the drumming, swallowing the splash of colors – how could you not? They stood enthralled. And more: they went up and talked to the performers, other kids their age, and were given gifts of stories about the regalia and the dances.

Then they found us: A group of girls decked out in beads and leather ran up to a pack of our students. Hugs all around. Smiling and chatter. Then I recognized the Ute Mountain dancers from our first night in Towaoc.

And then, again, between songs, the MC addressed us – even though I again had no idea how they knew who we were.

"We'd like to say hello to the students from San Francisco," the MC's amplified voice bellowed as he pointed over our way. It was obvious which were us. The crowd and dancers and drummers applauded.

A pause. Then the joke: "Hey, why don't you all come up here and do a two-step or something?"

Everybody there got it this time.

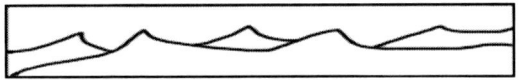

Men Gone Wild!

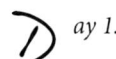 *ay 1.*

We gather at the river once again. Andy, Todd, and I roll down the gravel hill to the put-in and find another few of our crew there, boats out, gear strewn about.

Somehow every year it works.

See, there is little "plan," per se, to the annual Men's Trip. The idea is what's important. It's harder to catch catfish than to hook these guys: just trolling a vague, word-of-mouth meeting time and place – "mid-day at Sand Island" – for a month beforehand is enough to collect a stringer of men for three days every year. It's like the only plan is No-Plan.

This year waiting for us on the beach are the familiar figures of Eric, Randall, Ben, Dave, and Jan. First-timers Jared, Scott, and Jim are introduced. Wild Bill and a friend of his are supposed to arrive after dark – every year a group floats in on the night shift, under the nearly full moon – as long as the nasty weather dumping on the mountains back home doesn't discourage them.

We hope it won't, because here the weather has turned. After greetings, we make early-afternoon rigging toasts as the gently rattling November cottonwoods frame a clearing sky. By the time our convoy hits the river, the air is dry, the sun brilliant, and the headwind a spring-like breeze.

It seems that the Men's Trip No-Plan is working so far. Again.

I'm a firm believer in the kiva. I've had several: A 1980 Jeep Wagoneer. An old Chevy Van. A 10 x 12 cabin in a high mountain valley. A little room in my garage. I feel a deep kinship with those ancient male residents of the Southwest who negotiated with their wives for the first kiva. A hole in the ground with a stick roof? We can do that! And the women, too, I suspect, knew that this men-space was best for the whole tribe.

Todd knows what I mean. Although we don't really talk about it – we are male, after all – it's seems I always find Todd in whatever kiva is in my life at that time. One night sitting in my van parked in the middle of Ridges Basin, Todd came up with the idea of our investing in a fleet of "Chevy Kiva" rentals, so more men could explore their men-space callings affordably. Ken's Men's Vans, we'd call our "Men Business." It would be a service to society, we reasoned.

A van is nice, but my favorite kiva is a canoe. A 16-foot red tripping canoe, to be exact. And for the last few Men's Trips, in my river kiva Todd has been both bowman and barman, those roles overlapping and often indistinguishable. He is also the spiritual leader of the group: As we tie off our boats at our first campsite, Todd ascends the shore, like McArthur returning to the Philippines, and fastens a big pirate flag to the arm of a thick cottonwood.

There are laughs and more joking toasts to the flag, but I think he's got something here. Isn't the absolute value of piracy – the intent aside from the positive or negative manifestations – simply poaching your spirit from forces that would control it? The true Pirates – those we most admire safely from our side-line lives – are those who most deliberately and resolutely carve some space where they can assert their own style no matter what.

And that, right there, is both the function and beauty of the Men's Trip. Because here there's only one rule: Mutual non-coercion.

Moonlight sugars the smooth top teeth of the anticline rise across the valley. Around a campfire, groups of two or three cook a variety of meals. As pragmatic and efficient as it would be, there is, of course, no group-wide coordination of food, drink, cookware or appliances. This is understood and never discussed. It's one of those questions you just don't ask on the Men's Trip.

Todd, Andy, and I stand around a table and enjoy enormous

hunks of campfire-grilled steak, served communally on a tin plate with a side of baked beans bubbling over a backpacking stove. River knives and forks are the utensils. Dining is by headlamp and stars.

"This steak's a little raw," I mention politely to Chef Andy, as Todd and I check our fleshy slabs for signs of life.

"It's not raw steak," Andy retorts defensively. "It's cow tar-tar."

"Another Men Business," Todd suggests. "Beef Sushi."

Andy's the one who already owns a successful restaurant, so I let him tackle Todd's latest brainstorm. I have my own business to worry about.

A female friend told me once that I don't have enough women in my writings. But I argued that as a journalist valuing fairness and accuracy, I don't write about things I don't understand. But I mean no disrespect in this; in fact, I mean respect. Look, I think men and women are different. Very. But I also think this is not a bad thing – not in the least. In fact, I'm here to celebrate that.

"Too much beer, also," my literary-critic friend appended to her editorial feedback. "There's always too much beer."

To that charge I plead guilty. But I claim the fairness-and-accuracy defense again. Especially when writing about the Men's Trip, because the worst of what you might imagine is true: It's an unconscionable foray into excess. Hence, another thing you can't ask on the Men's Trip: "How many have you had?"

I've had a few by now. We all stand around talking. But this isn't "talking" like in mixed company, outside the kiva. When just men are together, it's the act of talking that matters. It's like the rap in hip-hop – you can listen, if you dare, but the real point of the nasty talk is musical.

As most of those stereotypes would predict, there is, of course, sexual undertones, and overtones, to everything. But don't get too excited; this stuff really isn't that different from hanging outside the gym at the junior-high dance. Suffice to say that for tonight, "mount" has become a remarkably versatile and amusing verb.

Also, when men gather in groups of just men, warmth and affection often manifest as bantering, badgering, and derogatory flagellating. This year, for example, everyone seems really glad Ben is with us, so "Ben, you suck!" has quickly become a rallying cry. It seems to bring us all closer together.

Still, though, sometimes sincere, touching compliments slip out. Like earlier today, when my relieving myself on the river's edge was cut startlingly short by a suddenly passing boat.

"Don't worry," Andy reassured me from nearby. "He just thought you were throwing him a rope."

Sometime around midnight I decide to give up on Bill and his friend arriving tonight, and wearily turn toward my sleeping bag on the river's edge. Before I wander down, though, I lean toward Todd.

"The No-Plan is unfolding perfectly," I tell him.

※

I startle awake. It's still dark. I turn and see the moon ready to plunge behind the ridge. It must be three in the morning.

"Get up you scumbags!" Bill's big voice booms from the middle of the wide, shallow river. A flashlight flashes, searching for the shore.

"Get up, you bastards! We're stuck in the mud!"

※

Day 2.

After a couple of hours on the water, we hit shore on river left, drag our boats up, and pull shoes from our drybags. While others mill around and set up lunches, Andy, Randall, Jan, and I head off on a run.

We do this every year: an hour-long sprint across broken-slick-rock desert, up and down steep arroyos, until we scramble up a great volcanic plug with a staggering view. It's dangerous and grueling, and my legs always come back shredded and stinging from dodging and leaping saltbush and sage. But it's so great.

This is another Man Thing, is it not? I don't mean to suggest that men are somehow tougher than women – fairness and accuracy wouldn't allow that. My wife runs at 6 a.m. every morning year round; I join her, only with great effort, once a year or so to show her I still care. And I've seen two babies come into this world, so I know first-hand that if men had to go through childbirth, cockroaches would already rule the earth. So it's something else.

I have a theory: Men are from Utah. Women are from Telluride.

I mean this metaphorically, of course. I propose that each place represents the topography of the psychology each gender generally inhabits. I also, though, don't mean this metaphorically at all.

Take the example at hand. For the Men's Trip, it's Utah: big, raw, wild, exposed. And we're all paddlers, so maybe this group's spirits and styles are best expressed in this canyon's entrenched meanders – seeking not, perhaps, the most direct route, but certainly the most lovely. Because to men, function is beauty.

For women, I propose, beauty is function. Several of the men on this trip have wives – also veteran river rats – who every year gather for their own Women's Trip. This, too, is a shameless foray into excess; but for the women, it is a carefully planned visit to a luxury hotel with posh amenities in classy Telluride. There, they savor saunas, pools, and masseuses. At night, they walk Telluride's scenic sidewalks and eat in nice restaurants and wander the fancy shops. And we men all strongly encourage, support, and assist our wives' carving out their own space in their own place. We think it's a good thing for the whole tribe.

I'll instead take this, though: The four of us claw our way up the crumbling volcanic tower and mount the summit (heh heh). Before us stretches redrock ridges and a brown belt of bare cottonwoods, through which threads the slowly sliding river. The dozen boats of our manly flotilla lie on the rocky shoreline below.

"Ben, you suck!" we bellow affectionately.

Day 3.

Morning. The campfire is rekindled. For breakfast, Andy, Todd and I hold bratwurst impaled on sticks over the flame. Meanwhile, we work on our retirement plans.

"I've got it: greeting cards for men," I announce. "We'd have three lines: cards men would send to men, cards men can send to women, and cards men would like to get from women."

"There's too few places that could legally carry any good ones," Todd notes, crushing our plan. We think some more while we roast our brats.

"Do you need a beer?" Andy asks politely. But I scold him: "You can't ask that on a Men's Trip. It's not about need. If there's a point to your drinking, you've got a problem. I *want* a beer."

He hands me one, apologizing. To avoid these conflicts in the future, we divert our attention to coming up with a list: The Top 10 Things You Can't Ask on the Men's Trip:

10. "Are you going to pick that up?"
9. "Can I borrow a mirror?"
8. "Did you wash your hands?"
7. "When will you be back?"
6. "Do these pile pants match my paddling jacket?"
5. "Did you fart?"
4. "Is there any Zima left?"
3. "Does this wet suit make me look fat?"
2. "What did you mean by that?"

And the no. 1 thing you can't ask on a Men's Trip: "What are you thinking?"

What I'm thinking, actually, is that as zany and crude as I make all this sound, to be fair and accurate about it, the Men's Trip is really more like "Boys Gone Mild."

Our after-breakfast activities illustrate this: Eric and Bill play golf (all sandtrap). Todd and I throw a baseball around. Others play a game of tug-of-war on milk crates. The guitar comes out and gets passed around: Dead music, Jimmy Buffett, some Pink Floyd, and, of course, a healthy helping of Neil Young – an honorary Men's Tripper. Andy, meanwhile, decorates the riverside with a lovely free-form arch of driftwood.

The truth is, we don't really need to act like stereotypical men all the time. And, the truth also is, we don't want to act that way at home or around women. It's just that, every now and then, it does our spirits good to pirate a visit to a kiva. It may not be pretty, but its function is its beauty.

And then?

After Utah, the best plan I can imagine is a visit to beautiful Telluride. And I mean that non-metaphorically. And metaphorically.

Chasing a stray baseball, I wander over and mention my new-found Men's Trip insight to Andy.

"Everyone here is really so nice," I tell him.

"Y'know what they say," Andy responds with a warmth only a man could understand, "if it's day three of the trip and you don't know who the asshole is, it's you."

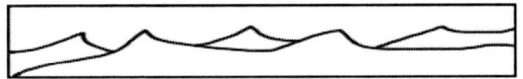

Soaking It In: A Love Story

So we got a hot tub.

Well, to be accurate, my wife got a hot tub. A nice one. A comfy six-seater with lovely cedar siding, a 220-volt heater, and 360 gallons of transparent blue-lit liquid delight.

And even though it's right there in our back yard, I, myself, don't really get it.

I guess it's me. I am and always have always been, even in the midst of my so-called "settled" years, more traveler than settler. I blame it on my Neanderthal Gene – some ancient recessive genetic remnant that flares up here and there in some of us more feral, less sedentary types. So even though at this juncture in my life I am, without doubt, more homeowner and townie than wanderer or way-farer, I nonetheless tend toward … well, sort of backpacking though this settlement. Which means that when it comes to domesticity, I am somewhat crippled – devoid of drive toward tilling the soil, dig-ging the garden, sculpting the yard, upgrading the car, or improving the home. Which means I seek to invest my time and resources into going rather than having. Which means that in my lifestyle, I tend to obsess on the life, often at the expense of the style.

Fortunately, those are Sarah's talents – she got the Civilized Gene.

There's no sarcasm here. While this might sound like the plotline of some predictable prime-time sitcom – that married-odd-couple shtick – I want to make clear that I am truly thankful for my wife's adeptness at modern domestic living. Even if that thankfulness sometimes comes reluctantly, hesitantly, begrudgingly.

Like now.

But I can forgive her this particular indulgence. She is, after all, a water girl: a former river guide, an active rafting parent, a paddler, a swimmer, a soaker, and a hot-spring connoisseur. So when our own local hot-spring-and-pool establishment changed hands and doubled its membership fee, she acted: She envisioned, plotted, studied, strategized, and struck. Even as I glowered and growled at this ... this Lake Powell right in my back yard ... this thumbs-up for coal-power steaming from the weeds behind my garage ... this posh accoutrement that I couldn't understand how we could afford – or, more, was embarrassed that we even owned – I had to admire her style, skill, and resolve in getting it done, even in the face of her husband's groaning and hand-wringing. She is a warrior of the homefront.

Beyond that admiration, though, I am left only to accept it.

But, I remind myself, acceptance lies at the heart of the traveler. A true traveler seeks to only see. To go. To do. To discover. To learn. To experience places and things and people as they are. So, as a bow to the spirit of the traveler I claim to be, I resolved, after the tub was set and the water was hot, to try to travel there, too.

And that's how I began soaking it in, in my own backyard.

It started with the moonlight, that ancient sentinel of the night surrounded by a thousand points of light – real points, and real light – shimmering high and far over the roof of the house, through the dark arms of the big blue spruces sprouting from between the houses and along the street of our downtown neighborhood.

Then it was daytime, and the sweet, dense, descending scent of the first of the season's lilacs that arced in a wave overhead.

And then it was the sounds of town. There was, of course, the passing of cars, the partying of the college kids down the block, the barking of the dog on the hill – the usual soundtrack of downtown life. But given enough time, other things began to rise to the fore, aural information usually lost or ignored in the hurrying around our home: the croaks of the ubiquitous, lordly ravens; the bantering and bickering of birds at the feeder; the rattling of the aspen – planted on the south side of our house a dozen years ago when Anna was born. Until then, until sitting quietly in that steaming water, I hadn't been aware of the subtle, alpinish sound of their quaking and shaking. I hadn't really noticed how tall they'd grown.

Like Anna and Webb.

I mean, I'd noticed how they'd grown – more than I noticed the aspen, of course. But this was different, this new sitting with our kids in our backyard in the new hot tub. This just loafing and soaking offered – or, perhaps, forced – us to just … face each other. To just … chat. Not "talk" – like, "Let's talk, son." But small talk. Casual, unforced, unrequired conversation laced with those quiet, comfortable pauses that, as my own dad pointed out to me once, really show how much you are connected to someone. In those words and pauses, in that just being there together, soaking and smelling and listening and looking around, I really noticed how big my kids have become. And how mature. And interesting. And pleasant. And thoughtful. And delightful.

So that's how I came to realize that, while sitting in a hot tub in my back yard is not traveling far, it's still traveling. It's still that traveler's space where, instead of forcing or forging experiences, you just experience.

That's how I also came to realize that this is Sarah's style of traveling: traveling the homefront.

Don't get me wrong: I, myself, still ache to *go*. To drive, ride, run, walk, or crawl away, out there, somewhere. I still hanker to see what it's like over there, to meet who's over there, to learn what's going on over there. Anywhere. And, too, I still twitch and twitter when it comes time to spend, build, upgrade, or in any other way to stay and not go away. We Neanderthal types just ain't good at that stationary civilized kind of stuff.

Meanwhile, in turn, my wife endures, and I think sometimes even appreciates, those things about me. Because they spice and balance her own home-style venturing with that wandering spirit and wayfaring perspective. That's what I hope, anyway. Because that's how travelers have to traveler together: individual journeys bound in shared adventure.

Like a well-traveled love. Because like traveling, an old love is not about loving someone for what they are, but as they are.

And tonight, out in the hot tub, I'm going to thank her for that.

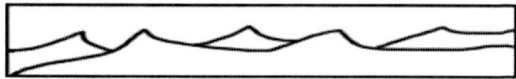

Gnawing the Bones

The little things? They aren't little.
John Zabat-Zinn

I'll admit it: Even after living in and wandering around Colorado for more than 25 years, I hadn't been there before. And even after some recent visits, I have to say that I still haven't been deep into the heart of it, or even seen much of it.

But my point is: I don't need to.

The HD Mountains fall away from the southwestern corner of the San Juans like a dangling foot. Low and rumpled, never rising anywhere near treeline, they stand like choppy water between the Piedra River on the east and the flat plain of Florida Mesa on the west, finally pinching out on the south on the shores of Navajo Reservoir, the sunken middle trunk of the San Juan River.

On the north, looming over and dwarfing the HDs, rise the massive ramparts of the greater San Juan Mountains – a landscape of ragged, jagged, snow-field-patched peaks and green, stream-laced alpine valleys. Dramatic and charismatic, the San Juans are given their due by being largely protected in perpetuity under the shield of the Wilderness Preservation Act, as the Weminuche and South San Juan Wilderness Areas.

As a relatively little landscape – only about 40,000 acres – the HDs remain little-known, little-appreciated, and little-visited. Few people outside of southwestern Colorado are aware of their existence

– for tourists, it's just a blank spot on the Rand McNally, and even those who do live here mostly know them as the area of rolling hills south of the highway when you drive between Bayfield and Pagosa Springs.

Little known, maybe; but they are also, remarkably, and importantly, little developed. In fact, RARE II, a government study in the late 1970s that inventoried the remaining roadless areas around the country larger than 5,000 acres, found 23,000 acres of the HDs qualifying as official Roadless Area designation. Other surveys claim as much as 40,000 acres – all but the outer foothills of the HDs – as defacto roadless area. Still, despite the RARE II findings, the Forest Service chose to not nominate the HD Mountains for protection when they had a chance under the Wilderness Act of 1980.

But lack of designation does not mean lack of value. Even though it is, by Colorado standards, a small range of mini-mountains, the HDs are vital to wildlife in southwestern Colorado because of their mostly undeveloped and largely-roadless nature and its unique mix of climates. The mountains, reaching only about 9,000 feet at their highest, are home to Blue spruce, Douglas fir, and Ponderosa pine, as well as pinion-juniper, scrub oak, and sagebrush. As such, the region provides healthy low-elevation wildlife habitat – a rarity, as this type of terrain is also prime real estate in a booming market. As a roadless area, the mountains serve as an undisturbed migration corridor linking the wild high country to the north with wintering grounds in the high desert to the south. The Forest Service even closes public roads in the area during the winter to create protected, quiet space for wildlife during this critical, sensitive time.

Recognizing these values, the 6,000-plus-acre Ignacio Creek drainage – the roadless heart of the roadless HDs – has been proposed as a Research Natural Area because of its pristine condition. Ignacio Creek flows south, onto Ute land, so the general public has not had access to the area. If they did, though, they'd find a valley harboring a legacy: stands of Ponderosa that have never seen ax or chain saw (the vast majority of Ponderosa pine in southwestern Colorado were logged and shipped away in the 19th century), including one stand of more than a square mile of several-hundred-year-old trees. Also, since the area hasn't been pierced by a road, the drainage is free of noxious weeds and non-native plants, and is home to two threatened species: the Mexican spotted owl and the Southwest willow flycatcher.

The area also contains at least 100 pre-Puebloan sites – which earned it a spot on the National Registry of Historic Places in 1983. Even the Southern Ute tribal council – no shy wallflower when it comes to resource exploitation – voted to not allow development on their portion of the HDs, recognizing the area as a sacred site.

A little place with big values.

Being "little" in so many ways, though, also means the HDs – unlike their more majestic and popular cousins to the north – are little protected. And so, recently the U.S. Forest Service and Bureau of Land Management opened the HD Mountains and its roadless area to oil and gas development.

The decision is the long-awaited outcome of the "Northern San Juan Coal Bed Methane Project." The project was begun following a 2001 proposal by six energy companies to drill 162 new wells and 107 miles of roads and pipelines in the northern San Juan Basin – an area of about 125,000 acres that includes the HD Mountains and Roadless Area, bordered by a northward-curving line running from southeast of Durango to Pagosa Springs, and down to the boundary of the Southern Ute Reservation. Included in this proposal was a road up Ignacio Creek for 24 wells and two compressor stations in the drainage.

After five years of study, meetings, and public input – 70,000 comments were filed on the draft Environmental Impact Statement alone, and five local governments passed resolutions favoring protecting the HD Mountains Roadless Area – the Final EIS was released in August 2006. Some of the issues cited in the EIS included property values, noise, visual impacts, tax revenues, water depletions, surface and groundwater impacts, gas seepage into domestic water wells, dying vegetation from seeping gas, harm to wildlife, the loss of roadless areas in the HDs, archaeological resources, and air quality.

All good, valid, tangible, rational concerns.

All ruled not worthy of stopping oil and gas development, even in the HD Mountains, even in the HD Mountains Roadless Area.

All, therefore, missing the big point about this little area.

⟋⟋⟋

Presently, the area studied in the Northern San Juan Coal Bed Methane Project has around 300 coal-bed methane wells and 200 miles of access roads and pipelines. The HD Mountains themselves are mostly undeveloped, but have some 20 gas wells and 15 miles of access roads and pipelines, generally on the western and eastern edges of the range.

The official Record of Decision is the final word on the issue. The final decision approved 127 new pads and 93 miles of new roads and pipelines in the northern San Juan Basin. (In addition, there are proposed another 100 well pads and 30 miles of road construction on private land, outside of the decision's jurisdiction.) The decision also approves 22 pads and nine miles of roads and pipelines in the HD Mountains Roadless Area (which the Forest Service now lists as 20,111 acres, despite a recent "citizen's survey" that still claims 39,000 contiguous roadless acres – an area slated for 30 wells under the decision).

Although this ruling is down from the 79 wells in the roadless area that was approved in the draft EIS, and rejects wells and roads in Ignacio Creek (until, at least, the industry improves its methods of drilling on steep and unstable slopes), the decision nonetheless opens 25 percent of the HD Mountains Roadless Area to the oil and gas industry, and leaves the door open for more wells and road building in the future.

⟋⟋⟋

The oil and gas industry's coveting of the HD Mountains is not new. As part of the oil-and-gas-rich San Juan Basin, they are hard to avoid – although they're also hard to access, which is why the HDs remain mostly undeveloped and largely roadless this late in the oil-and-gas game.

The San Juan Basin is an area along the northwestern New Mexico/southwestern Colorado border approximately 100 miles long by 90 miles wide. The large bedrock bowl provides a natural catchment for clean and versatile natural gas – and not-so-clean-and-versatile coal. This coal, though – found mostly in the swamp-turned-to-stone bedrock layer called the Fruitland Formation – is also itself a source of a particular form of natural gas called coal-bed methane.

Traditional natural gas is free gas held in place by impermeable bedrock layers, but coal-bed methane is chemically bound to coal. Because of its large internal surface area, coal stores up to seven times more gas per volume than a traditional gas pool. But while tapping traditional natural gas means essentially putting in a well and letting the gas rise, coal-bed methane production involves pumping massive amounts of groundwater from coal seams to release the gas, which leads to some unique challenges. Large amounts of groundwater, which is usually saline, must first be pumped from the coal seam to free up the gas. Once freed, though, methane gas can then migrate upward, following either bedrock fractures or the well's borehole itself, into homes or other aquifers. Also, once this dirty water – called "mud" – is pumped to the surface, it needs to be stored and disposed of, requiring additional facilities, activities, and impact areas, and sometimes leading to more areas harmed by accidents and contamination.

Today, the average American household burns 50,000 cubic feet of natural gas each year. Looking to meet this demand – and backed by a tax break for developing "unconventional" energy sources – there has been a boom in coal-bed methane as a source of natural gas since the mid1980s. Coal-bed methane now accounts for nearly 10 percent of the country's natural gas production; by 2000, the San Juan Basin already accounted for some 4 percent of the country's natural gas production and had become California's single largest supplier of natural gas. More than 25,000 wells were drilled in the San Juan Basin between 1921 and 1995; today there are more than 20,000 active wells in the Basin, and another 15,000 are planned.

The HDs themselves stand near the Fruitland Outcrop – where the Fruitland Formation reaches the earth's surface on the rim of the big bowl of the San Juan Basin – which means that here the gas held captive in the coal seam sits at a relatively shallow depth. For this reason, in the 1970s, the U.S. Geological Survey first identified the HDs as having potential for oil and gas development. In response, the Department of the Interior opened the mountains up for leasing from 1974 to 1984. Most of those leases, though, were never developed because of the rugged, steep terrain and the remote locations. Those that were developed in the 1980s and 1990s, mostly in the Saul's Creek drainage, east of Bayfield, and in the low foothills surrounding the mountains, were often met with protests and civil disobedience from a coalition of farmers, ranchers, hunters, backpackers, and wilderness advocates.

The main reason the oil and gas industry has thus far avoided the HDs, though, is because they are small in another way: They sit on top of just a little bit of natural gas. The HD Mountains are estimated to hold 87 to 118 billion cubic feet of extractable gas – less than the U.S. consumes in two days.

But now the oil and gas industry wants at the HDs because, when it comes to oil and gas, we're down to the little things. It's down to gnawing the bones.

Although production and development will continue for 30 or 40 years, most of the rest of the San Juan Basin has been tapped. According to the Colorado Oil and Gas Commission, between 2003 and 2005, the average take per well in the region declined by 10 percent and total production fell by 3.5 percent. Red Willow Productions, the Southern Ute Tribe's gas leaser and developer, first reported evidence of a decline to the Tribal Council in 1989.

I put these facts up there not for any sort of sign of coming cataclysm or indicator of any dramatic trend – but to point out the obvious: Oil and gas, like any "reservoir," any limited resource, is there, gets used, then is done.

Just like wild country. Like roadless country. Like the HDs.

The other obvious part, therefore, is: We're going to have to adapt to the end of natural gas at some point – and we will, because we're smart, resourceful, creative people. So the question then is: Where do we draw our lines? Where do we say, Enough – the inevitable is coming, so we stop here, we change now?

I say: How about we stop at the edge of wild country? At roadless country? At the HDs?

Look, I understand about law and management plans and the EIS process. But this isn't about due process or legality or economics or rights or even energy demand. This is about this: We are now gnawing the bones – the bones of our ancestral landscapes, and the bones of our unborn children. Now this is about something else. Now this has to be about something else.

Now the question is: Just how desperate are we?

Now the question is, not is it legal, not is it economic, not even is it feasible – now the question is, What are we leaving? What are we *not* doing?

And to do that, we need a consideration – even for a little-known, little-visited, little-appreciated little place like the HD Mountains – that goes beyond law, plans, economics, and technology. We need a reason to draw a line around the bones that are left.

I argue, We need to break the trance of our own present time and forge a re-enchantment with our children's children.

And for that, more than the glamorous, dramatic, well-known and well-protected landscapes, the bones matter. For the future, the little intact places that form the support skeleton of the world matter most. They're all we have left.

And for that – for them, those who will come after us, after the gas is gone and the world has been remade – we need to be willing to say, Enough. We will make the changes we will need to make someday anyway right now.

We need to be willing to say, Enough. There are some things we will not gnaw to death just for ourselves.

I realize this perspective lies outside the letter of the law, the math of profiteering, and the ability of technology to breach, but it seems to me that the HDs are the the living bones that keep our countryside structurally sound, healthy, alive. Just ask the elk, the deer, the bear, the Mexican spotted owl, the Southwestern willow flycatcher. Ask the last of the grandfather Ponderosa trees, hiding in the steep, deep valleysides of Ignacio Creek.

Ask our grandchildren's grandchildren.

To carve roads and puncture wells into the HD Mountains – whether or not we ourselves ever set foot in or drive our ATVs or trucks through those unglamorous hills – is like the crack addict raiding his kid's piggy bank for one more toke. It is not "like" – it actually is – us hydrocarbon drunkards raiding the family savings for one more night at the bar.

It's gnawing the bones of our children.

Or, it's the place to say we have the courage, will power, forethought, wisdom, vision, and respect to say, Enough. For them. For those besides us.

GNAWING THE BONES

I have never been deep into the HDs Mountains. But I don't need to.

That is exactly why they're valuable.

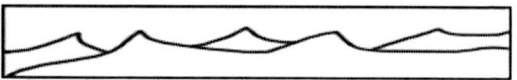

Lovers in a Dangerous Time

When you're lovers in a dangerous time
Sometimes you're made to feel as if your love's a crime.
Bruce Cockburn

I've got news for you: The West is not being loved to death. This, of course, goes against common wisdom and the constant keening of the mass-mediated modern West. There, the West is portrayed as a place where so many people have become so enamored of its open spaces, vast beauty, infinite variety and close-knit little communities that the land is being overrun by vision seekers via every conveyance possible: from foot to pedal to ski to motor to lift to helicopter to raft to jet-ski to houseboat. This, the sad tale goes, is destroying the fragile habitats that cover the dry West, whether that be mountain, forest, tundra, desert, chaparral, or even small town.

Many of these lovers of the West, the story goes, become so further enthralled with the place that they need their own first or second home here, which is so sacred it needs the grandest views, its own area of scenic open space, and, since it's certainly a power spot (not to mention a tax-deductible investment), it must have its own inherent mansion-esque grandeur.

Then there's those who love the West in a more straight-forwardly Machiavellian fashion: for the financial opportunities it offers them if they buy it, privatize it, invest in it, build on it, extract from it, expand upon it, or generally improve it toward our modern urban/suburban/industrial standards. Some of these free-market romantics love what they can get from here and bring elsewhere: the West's still-mostly-full cupboard of places to puncture for oil and gas, forests to fell, water to divert, coal and oil shale to gouge and scrape, and airspace to poison with radioactivity and power-plant emissions. And still others don't even need to come here: they're happy with a long-distance love affair with the West for its big, open and undeveloped spaces that can absorb the noxious, toxic, septic, plastic, packaged, airborne or otherwise unwanted wastes from those places already fully urbanized, suburbanized, and industrialized.

How much more of this loving can the West bear? the media cries. And rightfully so.

Well, not much, that's for damn sure. I'm with you on that one, brother. Here in my own beloved Four Corners region, some of that not-so-good lovin' includes a new four-lane highway to Albuquerque, a billionaire's plans for a mega-resort nestled between two wilderness areas, the coming of an enormous new power plant and powerline to Phoenix and Las Vegas, the return of uranium mining, the dewatering of a major river and the flooding of rare low-elevation elk habitat for a pork-barrel water project, a little ski area morphing into yet another world-class year-round destination resort (and the accompanying outbursts of condo developments rising like tumors among the trees in the dozen miles in either direction from there), and housing developments and trophy homes in every nook and cranny of every landform with improved-road access.

This love-fest afflicting the West has morphed into a full-bore greeding frenzy.

If you live here – and say you, too, love the West – you recognize this story and its familiar cast of characters: Your basic "loving the West to death" brought to you by the usual cabal of corporate raiders, real-estate pimps, stock-market carpetbaggers, and the hydrocarbon mafia. Capitalo-fascism from those who measure their love in dollar-investment-return and personal luxury.

Well, I make no claim to the name "expert" on the topic, but after thirty-or-so years of trial-and-error adventuring and learning in love and marriage, that to me ain't love. And no matter how busy and active and involved those people might be, I will dare to declare that they ain't the West's lovers.

Yes, lovers make use of each other – loving isn't a passive activity, and it is in many ways absolutely self-serving. In a relationship, each lover is gaining something valuable, even necessary. But a true lover doesn't exploit his loved the detriment of the other's health; and the truest lovers don't manipulate their loved ones to the point of harm of the other's truest, wildest, most natural self. A true lover doesn't seek to mold the loved to what he or she wants; a true love seeks only to see – to encourage, to embrace – what the loved most is, most needs to be, most can be.

No, the West is not being loved to death. It is being paved, developed, privatized, airported, resorted, second-homed, marketed, Mc-Mansioned, lift-served, Wal-Marted, reservoired, dug up, dumped on, energy-extracted, coal-fired, and uranium and gold and coal and oil-shale mined to death. That might be good for the investment portfolio …. But it ain't love.

Real lovers – lovers as "er"-ers, as people who *do* – know love is an action, not merely admiration. They know that this loving is a conscious, sometimes inconvenient, frequently unprofitable choice that sometimes demands restraint, respect and responsibility, and always requires reflection, vigilance, and a willingness to act to protect both the synergy that is being in love, and the symbiosis that is actually loving another.

Real love is a space where each lover is better, freer, wilder than they are anywhere else. And real lovers create and protect each other's space to be what he or she most is, where they're most healthy – even if it means restraint, or self-control, or even if what's best is to leave your beloved alone to go his or her own way. You don't prostitute your lover. You don't try to make your lover over. You don't work your lover to death for your personal hungers, needs, wants, or gain.

And real lovers don't let others do those to their love without a fight. Because inaction is an action; silence is a statement.

So here's what I want to know: Where are all of those West Needers – those truly out here, out there, because of what the West is – when it comes time to stand up to the West Bleeders – those who can only see the West in terms of what it can be made into, what it can make for them?

You're out there – boating on the rivers, fishing in the streams, hiking and biking and stalking game in the mountains, camping and climbing and canyoneering in the deserts. And you can do that because right around us, all around us, where ever we live out here, is big, open, and wild places. And lots of public spaces where we can get out and challenge ourselves and savor the land.

But where is the accompanying boom of people standing by the land that is the West? Where is the army of defenders fighting to keep the "public" in our public land?

Outdoor recreationists claim to love the West as well, and claim to do that in a way that doesn't ravage the land. And they preach the right to use the West's abundance of public lands. For too many, though, calories burned while playing is all the energy they have for the land. Or maybe a few bucks here and there for a membership in the Sierra Club or somesuch group.

My question is: Where are all these hordes of people we see out on the trails and in the mountains and on the rivers when the county commissioners meet to discuss development and road building and tourist marketing? When the Sierra Club actually has a person-to-person meeting? When some federal agency holds public meetings on land management? Where are their letters to the editor when the Bush Administration cuts budgets to the Park Service or to let the oil and gas industry run amok over BLM land or wants sell off our Forest Service lands? Because all this – and a helluva lot more – is happening right now.

It's a dangerous time. But where are the West real lovers now?

Out playing.

"Sentiment without action is the ruin of the soul," warned Edward Abbey. Love without loving is the ruin of your lover, says I. It's time to give back, folks. To be environmentally aware means to be environmentally active, and the right to use our public lands comes with the responsibility to do something for those lands.

Why? Here are few good reasons, just for starters.

Because recreation – and the places needed for recreation – needs to be recognized for its importance to Westerners. It's the nature of our present world: Although the land has a right to exist for its own intrinsic reasons, in modern society uses must justify themselves economically and politically. Here, silence is not golden, it's fatal.

Because recreationists need to improve their images. Believe it or not, some people think bicyclists are idiotic trail and road Nazis, that rock climbers are rude little children with no respect for private property, and that hunters are armed drunks. It takes effort to dispel these distorted images. It takes education. It takes involvement. Until then, expect more rules and regulations and lock-outs.

And lastly, the most obvious and moral reason: Because love and defense go hand in hand. Because once it's gone, it ain't coming back. Because if we don't do it, who will? Because our kids – and our kids' kids – are going to need these places, these sacred, sane spaces, even more than we do now.

So, sure, spend the day boating, floating, casting, climbing, wandering, riding ... then, sure, go drink a few beers at the pub sharing stories about your great days in the sun. But after that, there's that meeting to go to, that letter to write, that place to defend, the river to

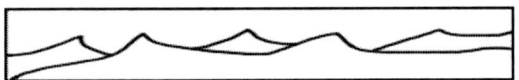

Third Party Candidate

Freedom is a psycho-kinetic skill.
Hakim Bey

*T*he following is the transcript of a stump speech delivered to no one in particular in Durango, Colorado, at the El Rancho Tavern, in the back corner near the foosball tables.

My fellow Americans, before I tell you about our new political party, I want to ask you: What is it that we want? And why don't we have it?

Simple questions. But the answers are complicated, aren't they? Or so we're told by our political, economic, academic, and celebrity leaders – those we look toward and have charged with the task of leading us to those things for us, those things we want, that we work toward, that we've always been working toward.

It's complicated, they say. It's complicated, we all say. That's why we haven't got it quite worked out. That's why we're not there ... yet. And they say, "That's why you need to re-elect us! That's why you need to pay us more! That's why you need to do what we say! Because we can get it done for you!"

Well, my friends, that's not what this new political party is going to say. Because this new political party really is going to show the way to those things. Because our candidates really know how to get them.

A toast, then! To our new political party!

(Pause for a long draw on a bottle of beer.)

So I ask you again: What do we want?

I'd like to posit a simple answer to that complicated question:

Happiness and security.

That's it really, isn't it? I mean, we are confronted with many ways of defining those things, and we're told endlessly of a vast array of ways of attaining them – do this, don't do so much of that, buy this, learn that, move there, own these, follow that program, behave this way, don't behave too much that way, be more like him, dress more like her, and always watch out for ... them.

Nevertheless, we know what we want. And that's why we elect, hire, pay, serve, and follow those powerful people: To carve for us the conditions we need to attain and retain our happiness and security. Which means ... if the circumstances for happiness are never really settled – because it's complicated! – and security is never really assured – because it's complicated! – then those leaders are also guaranteed jobs, are they not? Thereby assuring their own happiness and security – as they define it, as power and wealth.

The problem, though, my friends, is not our political leaders – hacks most of them are – or CEOs – not even the vilest lay-off-loving, pension-raiding kind – or even the prime-mortgage rates, or stock market, or politics, or education, or the decline of morality, or the rise of our enemies ...

The problem, I'm here to suggest to you, is nothing less than the very way we live. It's the nature of the beast in whose belly we reside.

(Short pause while shot glass is dropped into a pint of ale.)

But you'll never hear the other parties tell you that. Because their jobs are in the belly of the beast.

In this new party, though, we've redefined our jobs.

A toast, then, to doing our jobs!

(Longer pause for slamming of boilermaker, followed by a large belch.)

Happiness and security. That's all we ask.

To be happy means being free to be who you most are – who you cannot not be. It means liking where you are, physically, and to live days that are mostly meaningful, enjoyable, interesting, and relaxed. It means knowing what gives you satisfaction, and then doing it, and doing it well. It means having a role in a caring and meaningful and helpful alliance of kin and community.

Security means always having those things. Or, more to the point: security is understanding that the nature of Nature is that things change, shit happens, but still knowing – always, no matter what, no matter where, no matter when – that you have the skills to be yourself, to savor where you are, to do what you need to do to get by, and to find others to share with and care for.

Even here. Even now.

Of course, you won't hear the other political parties telling you that. They tell you we have two choices: Left? Or Right? Either way, they want to lead. And either way, neither path leads out of the belly of the beast that is our unstated rule that says we need to be led to happiness and security.

But our new party is neither left nor right.

And it's certainly not straight …

(Short pause for licking and then salting of thumb, and lifting of fresh shot glass.)

No. Our new party is forward. Right down the middle. Or off to the side. Or out into the woods – it's whatever route each of us needs to take to seek our own happiness, and to build the security that only comes by doing things for ourselves.

A toast, then, again! To finding our own way!

(Pause for licking of salt off thumb, shooting of shot, and sucking on slice of lime.)

My fellow countrymen, we were once wild. For millions of years, we were tribal hunter-gatherer nomads. It's how we evolved, because it's what worked the best for happiness and security – strong, unique selves; distinct days in powerful places; useful talents and valuable skills; and strong bonds with close companions. No wonder we still want those things – we might not be wild, but we are still those wild beings, even if we've been herded like domesticated sheep and cattle.

Oh, I'm sorry. It's PC to call it "civilized consumers and employees."

But there's something else our leaders, and textbooks, and media make sure we don't learn: We might not be wild, but like rez dogs and barn cats and dandelions that punch through even concrete, we can still go feral.

(Pause to accept fruity drink in shapely glass with umbrella sticking out.)

And so the Feralist Party is hereby established under only a single simple platform: Go feral!

Feralists may still seek to change things, but we don't *need* things to change. And we don't have to wait for circumstances to be "right."

Feralists are out to create new things entirely. All we have to do is dare to live differently, dare to live deeply, dare to take control of our living.

Dare to live at all. That's what Feralists do.

(Dramatic pause to stir cocktail with umbrella thoughtfully.)

I know, I know. It's election season, and you're sick of the posing and posturing and pandering of political parties working to garner your vote. So you must now think I want you to vote for somebody.

Well, my fellow Feralists, I'm here to tell you, we don't need no stinking election! Because in the Feralist Party, *you* are the candidate.

And you are already elected.

So go take office: in your own skin, in your home place, in your skills and talents, in your family and friends and tribe.

Where ever and whenever. Here and now.

Just go feral.

But first … a toast!

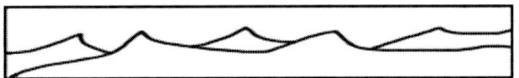

Pyrophilia

*I*t's a cold winter night. Yet my friend Todd and I sit outside. We haven't seen each other for a while, so we can think of no better location for a warm reunion than here in my cold backyard, under the moonless and star-filled night sky, sitting around a fire.

So that's what we do. We sit on lawn chairs and drink cold beers and watch the flames rise and spin and snap out of the incandescent pool of coals that we occasionally feed, when one of us feels the urge or need, with sticks or splits of logs. Sometimes we talk. But as much as we chat we also just sit and sip and silently share our staring at the fire and looking around at the street-lit neighborhood and the dark foothills around town and those ice-crystal stars whispering above us.

Nothing could be better.

We've passed a lot of time together around fires, Todd and I, in a number of places – my yard, his yard, on the river, out and about. And it's not only with Todd. In fact, twice this week already I've found myself around a backyard campfire, talking with friends, or toasting marshmallows for smores with the kids, or playing guitar with some buddies, or … just sitting and contemplating the red heart of the flames. In our tribe, campfires aren't only for the backcountry.

I can't speak for my neighborhood accomplices in regard to this on-going fire-affection, but in my case I can safely say that this pyrophilia is a congenital condition. It might seem like one of those "You know you're a redneck if …" jokes, but the fact is that my warmest and happiest memories of childhood revolve around evenings with my parents and their friends and kids encircling an altar-like concrete hearth my father had constructed in our backyard. While the grown-ups would sit around the fireplace and do … well, do whatever grown-ups do sitting around a fire (which, from my present adult standpoint, seems to be blessedly little), we kids would hang and join in the fire-lit conversation for a while, until we either sprinted away on forays to play games or moved down to the pier to cast into the dark lake for catfish, which we would then bring back to fry over the open flames in a skillet my folks kept nearby for just such needs.

To a kid, nothing could have been better.

Why is that? Kids, of course, cannot help but like the times they are physically surrounded by friends and family. But what about the actual fire itself?

In my office, I have a picture of my son at three years old. It's not one of those posed family-portrait images, but a candid shot that I like to think captures not so much what he looked like at that age, but who he really was. The picture was taken while we were camping in Utah, and in the photo Webb sits in a lawn chair that he himself had carried down to where we'd had a fire the night before. And that's it: He just sits there at a somewhat uncertain distance, staring at the site of the dead coals.

Looking at this image, I can't help but see him sitting there probing the space for whatever it was that had called us all to gather around that spot the night before. Or, perhaps, I sometimes think, he is also stalking whatever it was inside himself that impelled him to drag a chair down and sit quietly there that morning.

What is it about the campfire? Whatever it is, when I myself search for those callings, I find they arise from a past deeper than just my family. For at least a million and a half years, humans have used the campfire as the nexus of the family, the band, the tribe, of kin and community, of reflection and interaction. In fact, I would argue that around the campfire is where we actually became human – as the culture-makers we are, that one trait that truly separates us from other critters.

Because of that, the presence of a fire, I argue, triggers, like a spell, like an incantation, like a ritual, like some kind of ancestral Pavlovian response, both quiet introspection and convivial extraspection – those skills both conducive and essential to forging, negotiating, and reforming the understandings and relationships with ourselves and those around us that are our cultures. And the things that that don't come from the TV – the box in our living room, in all our lonely, isolated, individual living rooms, that substitutes for the campfire as the gravitational center of our modern family and social lives. That is our new wellspring of culture.

And I can't help but notice that when I see my now-teenaged son watching TV that he still looks a lot like that two year old in the picture – staring, processing, searching for ideas and understandings. But this replacement campfire burns in places that aren't real, surrounded by people who aren't really there, but who nonetheless have lots of things to say to him ...

So, when we recently reclaimed our backyard from our kids – now that they're teens it's time to toss the swingset, piece by dismantled piece, over the fence and downstream to the neighbors, for recycling and reuse by their two young kids – we went out and got a nice, big, steel firepan for our newfound space. This represents a small but significant evolution of culture in the Wright family, I think: I chose a moveable fireplace rather than building a nice stone one like my dad did so it, like the swingset, can become tribal property, moving around the backyards of our neighborhood.

Which it has a lot lately. Seems the tribe gets it.

Tonight, though, the firepan is home, where Todd and I share its joy and comfort on this chilly winter night.

After a while, Webb shows up, back from some high school activity, hanging with his own new and growing tribe. Like any teen, he quickly greets Todd and me as he trots by and heads inside. Probably off to watch TV or skateboard videos on the internet, I think.

Soon, though, he is back. He pulls up a lawn chair with us and casually starts poking the fire. And then tells us about his night.

Nothing could be better.

Postface

*Let the beauty we love
be what we do.*
Rumi

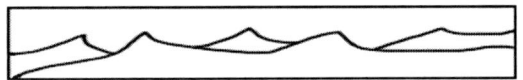

My Life Among the Tribe

This venture wasn't far, or exotic, or even all that rustic or challenging. In fact, it was downright posh. But it was still one of those welcome "Oh, yeah!" reminders of where we live and why we live here. All it took was two days with a dozen close friends in a ski hut high in the San Juan Mountains.

Colorado's high country is blessed with dozens of huts and hut systems spread across the state, and over the years, our group has tried many of them. Some with kids, some without; some for savoring slow cross-country skiing, some in search of pulse-pounding backcountry powder turns. This trip, though, was deliberately designed to appeal to our slothful, indolent, hedonistic sides. It was, after all, one of our compatriots' birthday.

For this visit we chose a cabin sitting at 11,500 feet above and behind Telluride Ski Area. It gave us what we were looking for: after earning our visit with a four-and-a-half-mile skin up a Forest Service road – all uphill, gaining some 2,000 feet – we arrived at a wood-and-stone cabin built on the site of an old mining generating station in the an alpine ghost town sitting beneath a ragged pair of 13,000-foot peaks.

Quaint enough. Inside, though, was the 21st century: full kitchen complete with microwave and coffee maker, bright living room with CD player and satellite radio, and several fun and funky bedrooms peaking with the third-floor "observatory" room. Oh, yeah: and there was a sauna and big, deep hot tub.

Needless to say, we didn't suffer. But, like I said, that's not why we were there, anyway.

One reason we were there was, of course, for the getaway from our work-a-day lives. It was a quick and easy jaunt: On Saturday morning, we delivered our kids to friends' houses for a couple of days, then we threw a bunch of our ski gear into day packs and were off. In two hours we were loading gear and shouldering our packs. Three hours after that we were resting our middle-aged bones, sitting around the hut drinking beer and listening to classic rock on the satellite radio and gawking at the alpine splendor cradling the cabin.

That, in a nutshell, explains why we all live here: so we can have this countryside and these adventures – even adventures in luxury, such as this – right here, right where we live. And the group in this hut is bound by each of our having chosen to eke out our livings in remote southwestern Colorado in order to have this quality of life – a "quality" based on where we live rather than as gauged by the quantity of income.

And we in this hut are bound by another choice.

Each of us here on this trip opted to raise their family in the Four Corners for the aforementioned reasons. Because we all wanted to offer our kids, not just a place to live, but a place to live in. A Place: a physical, tangible, meaningful landscape to not just grow up in, but to grow in: exploring and discovering, wandering through and wondering over, sharing powerful experiences, challenging themselves, changing themselves, together. And together, creating their own places, where they know they're insiders, where they'll have stories that mark their lives and their relationships, where they'll always know they're home.

And for the past decade and a half, the group in this hut has shared in each other's adventures in that Place-rich parenting, from strollers and backpacks, to feet and rafts, to skis and bicycles, to tents and chairlifts and huts …

But this time, there are no children. And that's another reason we're here.

No, it's not because we need to talk – what do you say when everyone knows pretty much everything about each other, talks every day, takes care of each other and each other's kids, has been through each other's best of times and worst of times? No, on this trip, there were few, or no, deep and revealing conversations. But that wasn't why we were there, anyway.

We were there to remember.

Because it's easy to forget. It's easy to forget in that so-called "real world," and in that bigger, louder, more pressing and much more depressing mediated world that comes in through our TV and radio and the internet and the pages of newspapers and magazines. When that tsunami of news and stress and information and demands washes over all that's right around, it's easy to forget that you still can choose good things, no matter what, even when so much seems to be going so bad. Because if you're looking out there, toward our institutions and leaders and businesses, for goodness, then you have forgotten the nature of economics and politics.

And of goodness.

You have forgotten that good things are not given, they are chosen.

And you have forgotten that only then – only with the abandon that comes with those choices – can you harvest the fruits or see the value of the things that can only be forged only over time. Landscape into Place. People into tribe.

And that's why we were there: to remember our tribe.

Not mere acquaintances, or even just friends. Not family – there is no blood between us. And not even community, or neighborhood, or partners, or buddies, or companions, or comrades in arms. Tribe: A relation based not on commitment, but on devotion; glued not by caution, but by caring; rooted not in information, but in immersion; shaped not by conformity, but by non-formality; steered not by judgement, but by knowing; sculpted not by ideas, but by experiences; seeing each other not with mere acceptance, but with sincere appreciation.

Tribe: strong collective through strong individuals.

Tribe: strong individuals through strong collective.

So we in this hut are bound by this choice, too. Because in this world we live in today you don't have to make this choice. In this world, you can choose to keep traveling. You can always start over somewhere else. It's encouraged, even – just look at what that so-called Real World is telling us all the time. At some point, though, each of us is forced – or offered, depending how you choose to see it – the opportunity to choose.

Neither choice here is good or bad, right or wrong – each is a valid choice. But this choice will define the rest of your life, and will define who you are the rest of your life. And if you're a parent, it will also define your kids' childhoods.

We in this hut have made our choices – to pass those things onto our kids: Place and Tribe. We have chosen those spaces where our kids know they'll always be accepted and appreciated, where they'll always be welcome, no matter what.

And for this tribe, that choice is our gift to our kids.

This binds us. As much as we shared this hike up here and this small space together, we have chosen to share the grander journey together in this shared place.

So on this hut trip, we didn't talk much. Instead, we laughed. Played cards. Told funny stories about our friend on his birthday. Drank and listened to music and soaked in the hot tub. We schemed ways to get our kids up here.

Through that just being together again, in this hut high in our beloved home mountains, we remembered why we're together, still. And we chose each other, again.

Illustrator, Designer, and Press

[Illustrator]
Bryan Peterson
www.draw-boy.com
bp@frontier.net

[Designer]
Lindsay James, elle jay design
www.ellejaydesign.com
lindsay@ellejaydesign.com

[Press]
Raven's Eye Press
Rediscovering the West

www.ravenseyepress.com

Printed in the United States
113804LV00002B/259-306/P